MUSHROOM
CULTIVATION
FOR BEGINNERS

TABLE OF CONTENTS

INTRODUCTION

Welcome to the intriguing universe of mycology, a realm brimming with enigma, allure, and practicality. This introduction is dedicated to every hobbyist gardener seeking new ventures, nurturing parents eager to share an enriching experience with their children, or food enthusiasts longing to infuse a personal flair into their culinary arts. *Mushroom Cultivation for Beginners* is the resource you've been looking for. Crafted with the novice in mind, this comprehensive manual requires no specialized tools or advanced methods.

Starting from the humble white button varieties gracing our supermarket aisles to the uncommon gourmet types, the edible fungi spectrum is broad and colorful. This guide will escort you through a captivating exploration of these unique organisms, their classifications, their roles in the ecosystem, and their utilization in gastronomy.

Mastering the art of cultivating these special organisms can be deeply gratifying. Imagine the sense of achievement when you create a dish using the fruits of your labor or when these mushroom wonders become a shared interest, resulting in precious memories with your family.

Mushroom Cultivation for Beginners extends beyond a guide; it's a route to forging an intimate bond with nature, witnessing the wonder of life's transformation from a simple spore to a mature fruiting body. We aim to walk you through every phase of the process, from choosing suitable varieties, understanding their lifecycle, and nurturing them to safely cooking and savoring your hard-earned yield.

Our expedition doesn't halt at cultivation. The manual is packed with practical guidance on processing, storing, and cooking your homegrown produce. It also furnishes you with the knowledge to identify and manage common diseases and pests that could hamper your endeavors.

For the adventurous palate or those with an entrepreneurial spirit, we venture into advanced techniques and shed light on commercial cultivation considerations. From hobby to potential enterprise, the opportunities are as expansive as the fungal kingdom itself.

We conclude our journey with a curated selection of scrumptious recipes and a detailed encyclopedia, ensuring this guide remains a reliable companion on your cultivation adventure.

Embarking on this path is not merely about growing food. It's about cultivating patience, instilling a sense of wonder, and appreciating nature's profound processes. So, don your gardening gloves and prepare to delve into the magical realm of fungi. Together, we will unveil the art of cultivation, turning this journey into an enriching experience for you and those dear to you.

PART 1

Chapter 1

THE WORLD OF FUNGI

MUSHROOM BIOLOGY

Fungi constitute a diverse and fascinating kingdom of organisms that play crucial roles in various ecosystems. When you hear "fungi," it's important to understand this refers to a wide array of organisms - from the molds growing on old bread to yeasts involved in fermentation, and from harmful pathogens causing diseases to beneficial types that help plants absorb nutrients.

Among the most well-known and captivating members of this kingdom are mushrooms. Now, it's critical to note here that while all mushrooms are fungi, not all fungi are mushrooms. In other words, "mushrooms" are a subset within the grand scale of the fungi kingdom. This difference is primarily due to the unique role and structure of mushrooms in the life cycle of certain fungi.

Mushrooms are the fruiting bodies of certain types of fungi. They are the reproductive structures that emerge from the soil or other substrates when conditions are favorable for their growth, much like apples on an apple tree. Their function is to produce and disperse spores, which can give rise to new fungal organisms.

The main body of a fungus, known as the mycelium, remains hidden underground or within the substrate. The mycelium consists of a network of thread-like structures called hyphae, which absorb nutrients from the environment. In everyday conversations and especially in culinary contexts, we typically refer to the visible, fruiting bodies as "mushrooms," while "fungi" is the term that encompasses the entire organism, including the often unseen mycelium.

Here are some key aspects of mushroom biology:

1. Structure

Mushrooms exhibit a distinctive structure consisting of a cap, stem, and often a ring or veil. The cap is the rounded or flattened top of the mushroom, while the stem provides support. The ring, also called the annulus, is a remnant of tissue that originally protected the gills or pores beneath the cap. The cap and stem are often different in color and texture, reflecting the tremendous diversity of mushroom species.

2. Spore Production

Mushrooms are responsible for spore production and dispersal. Spores are tiny reproductive cells that serve as a means of reproduction for fungi. They are produced in large quantities and are typically released from the gills or pores located on the underside of the cap. Spores can be dispersed by various mechanisms, including wind, water, or animals.

3. Ecological Roles

Mushrooms are vital for ecosystem functioning. They act as decomposers, breaking down organic matter and recycling nutrients. Many species form symbiotic relationships with plants, such as mycorrhizal associations. In these associations, the fungus and plant roots exchange nutrients, with the fungus aiding in nutrient uptake while benefiting from the plant's carbohydrates.

4. Nutritional Value

Mushrooms are a valuable food source for both humans and wildlife. They are low in calories and fat and rich in protein, fiber, vitamins (such as B vitamins and vitamin D), and minerals (such as potassium and selenium). Edible mushrooms are enjoyed in various cuisines worldwide and have been cultivated for centuries.

5. Medicinal Properties

Certain mushrooms possess medicinal properties and have been used in traditional medicine for their potential health benefits. For example, species like reishi (Ganoderma lucidum) and shiitake (Lentinula edodes) have been studied for their immunomodulatory, anti-inflammatory, and antioxidant properties.

6. Biodiversity

The kingdom of Fungi is incredibly diverse, with estimates of over 5 million species worldwide. However, only a fraction of fungal species have been described and studied, highlighting the vast potential for discovering new mushrooms and understanding their biology.

It's important to note that while mushrooms are fascinating and many are edible, it's crucial to exercise caution and seek expert guidance before consuming wild mushrooms. Some species can be toxic or deadly if ingested.

The biology of mushrooms encompasses a wide array of species, each with its unique characteristics, ecological roles, and potential applications. Continued research into fungi and mushrooms promises to uncover further insights into their biology, ecological significance, and potential benefits for human health and the environment.

EDIBLE MUSHROOMS TYPES

There are numerous types of edible mushrooms enjoyed by people around the world. Here are some popular and widely recognized edible mushroom varieties:

1. Button Mushroom (Agaricus bisporus)

The button mushroom is one of the most commonly consumed mushrooms worldwide. It has a mild flavor and a firm texture. As it matures, it develops into a larger mushroom known as the cremini or portobello. Button mushrooms are commonly found in grocery stores and used in a variety of dishes.

2. Shiitake Mushroom (Lentinula edodes)

Originating from East Asia, shiitake mushrooms have a rich, earthy flavor and a meaty texture. They are widely used in Asian cuisine and are also available dried.

3. Oyster Mushroom (Pleurotus ostreatus)

Oyster mushrooms have a delicate flavor and a tender texture. They are named for their resemblance to oyster shells. Oyster mushrooms come in various colors and are known for their versatility in cooking for stir-fries, soups, and sautés.

4. Portobello Mushroom (Agaricus bisporus)

Portobello mushrooms are mature button mushrooms that have grown to a larger size. They have a meaty texture and a robust flavor. Portobello mushrooms are often used as a vegetarian alternative to burgers or as a hearty ingredient in various dishes.

5. Chanterelle Mushroom (Cantharellus spp.)

Chanterelles are highly prized for their unique flavor, which is described as nutty and fruity. They have a distinctive funnel-like shape, a vibrant orange or yellow color, and a firm texture. Chanterelles often forage in forests and are often used in gourmet dishes, sauces, and risotto.

6. Morel Mushroom (Morchella spp.)

Morels have a distinctive appearance, with their cone-shaped caps covered in a honeycomb-like pattern. They have a rich, earthy flavor and are considered a delicacy. Morels are typically found in spring and are often sautéed or used in gourmet dishes.

7. Porcini Mushroom (Boletus edulis)

Porcini mushrooms are highly regarded for their intense flavor and aroma. They have a firm texture and a rich, nutty taste. Porcini mushrooms are available fresh or dried and are commonly used in Italian and Mediterranean cuisine, particularly in risotto and pasta dishes.

8. Maitake Mushroom (Grifola frondosa)

Maitake mushrooms, also known as "hen of the woods," have a distinctive frilly appearance. They have a robust flavor and a firm, meaty texture. Maitake mushrooms are often used in Asian cuisines and are also sought after for their potential health benefits.

9. Cremini Mushroom (Agaricus bisporus)

Cremini mushrooms are similar to button mushrooms but have a deeper flavor and a slightly firmer texture. They are often used in soups, stews, and sautés.

10. Enoki Mushroom (Flammulina velutipes)

Enoki mushrooms have long, slender stems and small caps. They have a mild, slightly sweet flavor and a crisp texture. Enoki mushrooms are commonly used in Asian soups, stir-fries, and salads.

These are just a few examples of common edible mushrooms, but there are many more varieties enjoyed by people worldwide. While these mushrooms are generally considered safe and delicious, it is essential to properly identify and prepare them. If you are unsure about a mushroom's edibility or have concerns, it is advisable to seek guidance from experts or consult reputable field guides to avoid any risks associated with toxic or poisonous mushrooms.

Exotic Edible Mushrooms

1. Matsutake Mushroom (Tricholoma matsutake)

Highly prized in East Asian cuisine, matsutake mushrooms have a distinct spicy-aromatic flavor and are often used in soups, stir-fries, and rice dishes. They are particularly popular in Japanese cuisine.

2. Lion's Mane Mushroom (Hericium erinaceus)

Lion's Mane mushrooms have a distinctive appearance with their cascading, white, icicle-like spines. They have a delicate, seafood-like flavor and a tender texture. Lion's Mane mushrooms are used in various dishes, including vegetarian and vegan substitutes for seafood.

3. Black Truffle (Tuber melanosporum)

Black truffles are highly valued for their intense, earthy aroma and flavor. They grow underground in association with certain tree roots and are often harvested with the help of trained dogs or pigs. Black truffles are used sparingly and added to dishes like pasta, risotto, and sauces to enhance their flavors.

4. Yellowfoot Mushroom (Craterellus tubaeformis)

Also known as winter chanterelles or funnel chanterelles, yellowfoot mushrooms have a delicate, fruity flavor reminiscent of apricots. They have a trumpet-like shape and a golden-yellow color. Yellowfoot mushrooms are used in sauces, sautés, and soups.

5. Hen of the Woods (Grifola frondosa)

Hen of the Woods mushrooms, also called maitake mushrooms, have a ruffled appearance and a rich, earthy flavor. They have a meaty texture and are used in stir-fries, soups, and sauces. Hen of the Woods mushrooms are also valued for their potential health benefits.

6. Porcini Mushroom (Boletus edulis)

Although porcini mushrooms were mentioned in the previous response, they deserve mention in the exotic category due to their popularity and culinary significance. They have a robust, nutty flavor and a firm texture. Porcini mushrooms are widely used in Italian cuisine, particularly in pasta dishes, risotto, and sauces.

7. Lobster Mushroom (Hypomyces lactifluorum)

The lobster mushroom is not actually a distinct species but a result of a parasitic fungus infecting other mushrooms, typically Russula or Lactarius species. It has a vibrant orange color and a seafood-like flavor. Lobster mushrooms are often used in seafood-inspired dishes or vegetarian alternatives to seafood.

8. Bamboo Mushroom (Phallus indusiatus)

Bamboo mushrooms have a unique appearance, with a long, slender stalk topped by a lacy, net-like structure called the indusium. They have a delicate flavor and are commonly used in stir-fries, soups, and Asian dishes.

These are just a few examples of exotic edible mushrooms, each with its own distinct characteristics and culinary applications.

Culinary Uses of Mushrooms

Mushrooms are incredibly versatile ingredients in the culinary world, offering a range of flavors, textures, and culinary possibilities. Here are some common culinary uses of mushrooms:

1. Mushroom Stir-Fries and Sautéed Mushrooms

Mushrooms bring a unique blend of taste and texture to various culinary applications, from stir-fries to sautéed delights. As excellent additions to stir-fries, they provide a meaty texture and have an uncanny ability to absorb flavors from accompanying vegetables and sauces. Quickly cooking them with ingredients like bell peppers, broccoli, and soy-based sauces can create a delightful and hearty dish.

On the other hand, sautéing mushrooms is another popular cooking method that truly accentuates their rich flavors and enhances their natural umami taste. Sautéed mushrooms serve as a versatile component in numerous dishes. They can be enjoyed as a standalone side dish, mixed into pasta or rice dishes for a flavor boost, used as a gourmet pizza topping, or elegantly served as a garnish for steaks and other meats. Both these cooking techniques demonstrate the incredible culinary potential that mushrooms offer.

2. Mushroom Soups

Mushrooms are often used as a key ingredient in creamy mushroom soups. They can be sautéed, pureed, or added as sliced pieces to create a hearty and flavorful soup. Mushroom soups can be enjoyed as a starter or as a comforting main course.

3. Mushroom Risottos

Mushrooms, such as porcini or shiitake, add depth and richness to risottos. Sautéed mushrooms are often combined with Arborio or other short-grain rice, creating a creamy and savory dish.

4. Stuffed Mushrooms

Large mushroom caps, such as portobello or cremini, can be stuffed with various fillings like breadcrumbs, cheese, herbs, and other ingredients. Stuffed mushrooms are typically baked or grilled until the filling is golden and the mushrooms are tender.

5. Mushroom Gravies and Sauces

Mushrooms can be used to prepare flavorful gravies and sauces. Sautéed mushrooms can be combined with broth, wine, cream, or other ingredients to create delicious sauces that complement dishes like roasted meats, pasta, and vegetables.

6. Mushroom Toppings

Mushrooms make fantastic toppings for pizzas, burgers, and sandwiches. Sliced or sautéed mushrooms add a savory and satisfying element to these dishes.

7. Mushroom Duxelles

Duxelles is a mixture of finely chopped mushrooms, onions, herbs, and sometimes bacon or shallots. It is used as a filling or a flavoring ingredient in various dishes, including stuffed meats, omelets, quiches, and pastries.

8. Mushroom Pâtés and Spreads

Mushrooms, when finely chopped or pureed, can be used to create flavorful pâtés and spreads. These can be enjoyed as appetizers or used as a sandwich filling or a topping for crostini or crackers.

9. Mushroom-based Vegetarian and Vegan Dishes

Mushrooms are often used as meat substitutes in vegetarian and vegan cuisine. Their meaty texture and umami flavor makes them suitable for dishes like mushroom burgers, mushroom-based "meatballs," mushroom stir-fries, and more.

These are just a few examples of the culinary uses of mushrooms. The versatility of mushrooms allows them to be incorporated into various dishes, adding depth, flavor, and texture. Exploring different cooking techniques and flavor combinations can reveal the true culinary potential of mushrooms in both vegetarian and non-vegetarian cuisine.

Fungi form a fascinating kingdom of organisms with diverse biology. Within this kingdom, mushrooms stand out as captivating and edible representatives. Mushrooms are the fruiting bodies of certain fungi, emerging above ground to release spores for reproduction. While the mushrooms themselves are highly valued for their culinary uses, it is important to understand the broader context of fungi in ecosystems.

Fungi play vital roles in the environment as decomposers, breaking down organic matter and recycling nutrients. They form symbiotic relationships with plants, aiding in nutrient uptake and promoting plant growth. Additionally, some fungi have medicinal properties and are being explored for their potential health benefits.

Among the various types of edible mushrooms, there is a wide range of flavors, textures, and culinary applications. Common edible mushrooms like button mushrooms, shiitake mushrooms, and oyster mushrooms are widely enjoyed and incorporated into a variety of dishes. Exotic edible mushrooms such as matsutake, lion's mane, and black truffles offer unique flavors and are sought after in gourmet cooking.

Mushrooms can be sautéed, used in soups and sauces, stuffed, added to risottos and stir-fries, or used as toppings for various dishes. Their umami-rich taste and diverse textures provide depth and complexity to culinary creations. Mushrooms also serve as a versatile ingredient in vegetarian and vegan dishes, offering a meaty substitute in recipes.

While mushrooms captivate our palates, it is essential to recognize their broader ecological significance and the need for responsible foraging or cultivation. Proper identification and caution should be exercised when consuming wild mushrooms to ensure safety.

Understanding the biology of fungi and exploring the world of edible mushrooms not only enhances our culinary experiences but also deepens our appreciation for the intricate roles these organisms play in ecosystems. The study of fungi and their culinary uses continue to expand, offering new insights, flavors, and potential benefits for both our plates and the natural world.

Chapter 2

GETTING STARTED WITH MUSHROOM CULTIVATION

Mushroom cultivation requires specific equipment and supplies to ensure successful growth and harvest. In this chapter, we will discuss the essential items you need to get started with mushroom cultivation and how to choose quality supplies.

BASIC EQUIPMENT AND SUPPLIES

List of Equipment

To embark on your mushroom cultivation journey, it is important to have the necessary equipment to ensure successful growth and harvest. Here is a more detailed list of the essential equipment you will need:

1. Growing Containers: Select appropriate containers based on the type of mushrooms you plan to cultivate. Common options include plastic trays, bags, or buckets. Ensure that the containers are clean and sterilizable to prevent contamination.

2. Substrate: The substrate serves as the growing medium for mushrooms. Depending on the mushroom species, you will need specific substrates such as straw, wood chips, sawdust, or a combination of these. It is possible to purchase a pre-sterilized substrate or prepare and sterilize it yourself using a pressure cooker or autoclave.

3. Spawning Equipment: Spawning involves introducing mushroom spores or mycelium into the substrate to initiate growth. You will need the following tools for inoculation:

   a. Syringes: Used to inject spore solution or liquid mycelium into the substrate.

   b. Scalpel or Razor Blades: Essential for cutting and handling mushroom cultures or agar media.

   c. Inoculation Loops: Small metal loops are used to transfer mycelium from the culture to the substrate.

4. Incubation Chamber: An incubation chamber provides controlled conditions for the mycelium to colonize the substrate. Consider the following equipment for creating an incubation chamber:

   a. Plastic Containers: Clean, food-grade plastic containers with lids are commonly used. Ensure they are large enough to accommodate the growing containers and provide adequate airflow.

   b. Thermometer: Use a digital thermometer to monitor the temperature within the incubation chamber.

   c. Heating Mat: If necessary, use a heating mat to maintain the desired temperature range for optimal mycelium growth.

5. Fruiting Chamber: Once the mycelium has colonized the substrate, mushrooms require a different set of conditions for fruiting. Consider the following equipment for creating a fruiting chamber:

   a. Plastic Greenhouse or Terrarium: Use a clean, transparent plastic structure to house the fruiting containers. It should provide ample space and ventilation for mushroom development.

b. Humidifier: Install a humidifier to maintain the required humidity levels within the fruiting chamber.

c. Hygrometer: Use a digital hygrometer to monitor and adjust the humidity levels accurately.

6. Lighting: While mushrooms do not require direct sunlight, they need a light source to trigger fruiting. Consider the following lighting options:

a. Fluorescent Lights: Choose cool white or daylight fluorescent tubes, which emit the appropriate spectrum for mushroom growth.

b. LED Lights: LED grow lights are energy-efficient and can be customized to provide the ideal light spectrum for mushroom cultivation.

7. Hygrometer and Thermometer: These devices are essential for monitoring and maintaining the proper temperature and humidity levels in your growing area. Opt for digital versions for accurate readings.

8. Cleanliness Supplies: Maintaining a clean and sterile environment is crucial for successful mushroom cultivation. Ensure you have the following supplies:

a. Disinfectants: Use a suitable disinfectant to clean and sterilize surfaces, tools, and containers.

b. Gloves and Masks: Wear disposable gloves and masks to prevent contamination and protect yourself during the cultivation process.

c. Clean Towels: Have a supply of clean towels or paper towels for wiping and drying surfaces.

d. Isopropyl Alcohol: Use isopropyl alcohol to sanitize tools and surfaces before working with mushrooms.

Having the necessary equipment will set you up for a smooth and successful mushroom cultivation journey. Ensure that all equipment is of good quality, clean, and properly maintained to maximize your chances of achieving healthy mushroom growth and bountiful harvests.

Choosing Quality Supplies

Selecting high-quality supplies is essential for successful mushroom cultivation. Here are some key considerations to help you choose the best quality equipment and materials:

1. Substrate Quality: If you are purchasing pre-sterilized substrate, ensure it comes from a reputable supplier. Look for substrates that are specifically formulated for mushroom cultivation and are free from contaminants. Check for consistent moisture content, as improper moisture levels can lead to mold growth or poor mushroom development.

2. Spawn Quality: Mushroom spawn is available in various forms, such as spores or mycelium on a substrate. When purchasing spawns, choose a reliable supplier known for providing

high-quality and viable spawns. The spawn should be free from contamination and have strong, healthy mycelium growth.

3. Container Durability: Select containers that are durable and can withstand the sterilization process. Opt for food-grade containers to ensure they are safe for mushroom cultivation. Check for any cracks, leaks, or signs of wear that may compromise the integrity of the containers. Sturdy containers will withstand repeated use and are easier to clean and sterilize.

4. Lighting Efficiency: When choosing to light for your growing area, consider energy-efficient options that emit the appropriate spectrum of light for mushroom growth. LED lights are popular choices due to their efficiency, customizable spectrum, and long lifespan. Look for lights specifically designed for horticultural use or with a color temperature in the range of 5000-6500 Kelvin.

5. Humidifier Reliability: Invest in a humidifier that is reliable and can maintain consistent humidity levels within your growing area. Read customer reviews and choose a model that is known for its durability and ease of maintenance. Look for features such as adjustable humidity settings, automatic shut-off, and easy-to-clean components.

6. Cleanliness Supplies: Ensure that your cleanliness supplies are effective in creating and maintaining a sterile environment. Choose disinfectants that are specifically formulated for killing a broad spectrum of microorganisms. Check the product labels for instructions on proper usage and dilution ratios. Use gloves, masks, and clean towels made of materials that do not shed particles or fibers, minimizing the risk of contamination.

7. Supplier Reputation: When purchasing equipment and supplies, consider the reputation of the supplier. Look for established companies or reputable online retailers known for providing quality products. Read customer reviews and testimonials to gauge the experiences of other mushroom cultivators. Seek recommendations from experienced growers or join online communities dedicated to mushroom cultivation to get insights into reliable suppliers.

8. Personal Experience and Feedback: As you gain experience in mushroom cultivation, you will develop preferences for specific brands or suppliers based on your own observations and results. Keep a record of the performance and quality of the supplies you use. Experiment with different brands and materials to find what works best for your specific cultivation methods and mushroom species.

By prioritizing quality supplies, you set yourself up for success in mushroom cultivation. Quality materials will contribute to a healthy growing environment, minimize the risk of contamination, and maximize your chances of obtaining abundant and high-quality mushroom yields.

SETTING UP YOUR MUSHROOM GROWING AREA

Creating the right growing environment is crucial for the successful cultivation of mushrooms. Whether you choose an indoor or outdoor growing area will depend on the type of mushrooms you plan to grow and the available space. Let's explore both options.

Indoor Growing Area

Indoor cultivation provides a controlled environment for mushroom growth, allowing you to regulate crucial factors such as temperature, humidity, and lighting. It is a popular option for cultivating a wide variety of mushrooms. Let's delve into the details of setting up an indoor growing area and explore some mushrooms that thrive in this environment.

1. Choose a Suitable Space: Select a room or an area in your home or a dedicated structure like a greenhouse or basement for your indoor growing area. Consider the available space, accessibility, and number of mushrooms you intend to cultivate. Ensure the space can accommodate the necessary equipment, shelves, and growing containers.

2. Clean and Prepare the Area: Before setting up your indoor growing area, it is crucial to clean and disinfect the space thoroughly. Remove any dust, dirt, or debris that could potentially introduce contaminants. Clean the walls, floors, and surfaces using a suitable disinfectant to create a sterile environment.

3. Ensure Proper Ventilation: Proper air circulation is essential for maintaining optimal conditions and preventing the buildup of carbon dioxide and stagnant air. Install fans or ensure the room has adequate ventilation to promote fresh air exchange and prevent the accumulation of moisture.

4. Install Lighting: Mushrooms do not require direct sunlight but need a light source to trigger fruiting and promote healthy growth. Depending on the type of mushrooms you plan to cultivate, you can use artificial lighting. Consider fluorescent or LED lights, as they are energy-efficient and emit the appropriate spectrum of light for mushroom growth. Position the lights at an appropriate distance from the growing containers to provide adequate illumination.

5. Set Up Shelves or Racks: Utilize shelves or racks to maximize the vertical space in your indoor growing area. This allows for efficient use of the available space and provides ample room for your growing containers. Ensure the shelves or racks are sturdy enough to support the weight of the containers and allow for proper airflow around them.

6. Install the Incubation and Fruiting Chambers: Dedicate specific areas within your indoor growing area for the incubation and fruiting stages. You can create these chambers using clean plastic containers or repurposed clean containers. The incubation chamber is where the mycelium colonizes the substrate, while the fruiting chamber is where mushrooms develop.

7. Control Temperature and Humidity: Mushrooms have specific temperature and humidity requirements for optimal growth. Use a digital thermometer and hygrometer to monitor and adjust the temperature and humidity levels within the growing area. Depending on the mushroom species, you may need to use heating mats, coolers, or humidifiers to maintain the desired conditions.

Now, let's discuss some mushrooms that thrive in indoor environments:

1. White Button Mushrooms (Agaricus bisporus): White button mushrooms are one of the most commonly cultivated mushrooms. They grow well in controlled indoor environments with temperatures between 55-70°F (13-21°C). These mushrooms are typically cultivated on composted substrates, such as a mixture of straw, manure, and other organic materials.

2. Oyster Mushrooms (Pleurotus spp.): Oyster mushrooms are known for their vibrant colors and delicate flavors. They are well-suited for indoor cultivation. Oyster mushrooms prefer temperatures between 65-75°F (18-24°C) and higher humidity levels. They can be grown on a variety of substrates, including straw, sawdust, or coffee grounds.

3. Shiitake Mushrooms (Lentinula edodes): Shiitake mushrooms are highly prized for their meaty texture and rich flavor. They can be cultivated indoors with temperatures between 55-75°F (13-24°C) and moderate humidity levels. Shiitake mushrooms are typically grown on hardwood logs or supplemented sawdust blocks.

4. Lion's Mane Mushrooms (Hericium erinaceus): Lion's Mane mushrooms have a unique appearance with their cascading white spines. They are gaining popularity for their potential health benefits. Lion's Mane mushrooms can be cultivated indoors with temperatures between 60-75°F (15-24°C) and higher humidity levels. They are often grown on supplemented sawdust blocks or hardwood substrates.

Outdoor Growing Area

Outdoor cultivation offers unique opportunities for growing mushrooms, particularly for species that require specific environmental conditions or naturally grow on trees and logs. Setting up an outdoor growing area requires careful consideration of factors such as location, substrate preparation, and mushroom species suitability. Let's explore the details of creating an outdoor growing area and discuss some mushrooms that thrive in this environment.

1. Choose the Right Location: Select an outdoor location that provides the ideal conditions for your chosen mushroom species. Consider factors such as sunlight exposure, shade, moisture levels, and soil composition. Different mushrooms have different preferences, so choose a location that matches the specific requirements of the mushrooms you intend to cultivate.

2. Prepare the Growing Beds: Prepare the soil or growing beds to create a favorable environment for mushroom growth. Remove any weeds, rocks, or debris that may hinder mushroom development till the soil improves its texture and create a loose, well-draining bed for the mushrooms.

3. Construct Shade Structures: If the selected outdoor area receives excessive sunlight, construct shade structures to protect the mushrooms from direct sunlight. Use shade cloth or natural materials like bamboo to create a partially shaded environment that mimics the preferred light conditions of the mushroom species.

4. Create Inoculation Sites: For mushrooms that grow on logs or wood chips, create inoculation sites by drilling holes or cutting grooves. This provides a suitable environment for the mushroom mycelium to colonize the substrate. The size and spacing of the inoculation sites will depend on the specific mushroom species and the substrate being used.

5. Inoculate the Substrate: Introduce mushroom spawn or mycelium into the prepared substrate. Follow the specific instructions provided for the mushroom species you are cultivating. Ensure proper spacing and distribution of the spawn or mycelium to facilitate even colonization.

6. Maintain Moisture Levels: Regularly water the growing beds to maintain the required moisture levels for optimal mushroom growth. Depending on the mushroom species and weather conditions, you may need to adjust the watering frequency and amount. Mulching the beds with organic materials like straw or wood chips can help retain moisture and regulate temperature.

7. Monitor and Protect: Keep a close eye on your outdoor growing area and monitor for pests, diseases, and changes in weather conditions. Protect the mushrooms from animals, excessive rainfall, and extreme temperature fluctuations. Take necessary measures to prevent contamination and ensure the health of your mushroom crops.

Now, let's discuss some mushrooms that can thrive in outdoor environments:

1. Wine Cap Mushrooms (Stropharia rugosoannulata): Wine Cap mushrooms are known for their rich, wine-colored caps and earthy flavor. They are well-suited for outdoor cultivation. These mushrooms prefer growing in wood chips or garden beds with rich, organic matter. They thrive in temperate climates and can tolerate a wide range of moisture levels.

2. Morel Mushrooms (Morchella spp.): Morel mushrooms are highly sought after for their unique appearance and delicate flavor. They are typically found in the wild but can be cultivated outdoors. Morels have a symbiotic relationship with certain tree species, such as oak, ash, and elm. Creating a suitable outdoor habitat with the right tree species and soil conditions can potentially yield successful Morel cultivation.

3. Chicken of the Woods (Laetiporus spp.): Chicken of the Woods mushrooms are vibrant, shelf-like fungi with a taste reminiscent of chicken. They grow on decaying hardwood logs or stumps. Outdoor cultivation involves inoculating logs with Chicken of the Woods spawn and providing the appropriate moisture and shade conditions.

4. Reishi Mushrooms (Ganoderma lucidum): Reishi mushrooms are renowned for their potential health benefits and adaptability to different growing conditions. They can be cultivated on logs or wood chips outdoors. Reishi mushrooms prefer shaded environments and humid climates.

These are just a few examples of mushrooms that can be successfully cultivated indoors and outdoors. It is important to research the specific requirements of the mushroom species you intend to grow and tailor your indoor/outdoor growing area accordingly. With proper care and attention to environmental conditions, you can enjoy a rewarding indoor mushroom cultivation experience.

Chapter 3

THE CULTIVATION PROCESS

CHOOSING AND HANDLING SPAWN

Spawn is a crucial element in the mushroom cultivation process. In this chapter, we will explore the importance of spawn, how to understand it, and the best practices for purchasing and handling spawn.

Understanding Spawn

Spawn plays a crucial role in mushroom cultivation as it serves as the inoculum for the growth of mushrooms. Understanding the different forms of spawn and their characteristics is essential for successful cultivation. Let's explore the various types of spawns and their significance in the cultivation process.

1. Spores: Spores are the reproductive units produced by mushrooms. They are microscopic in size and usually dispersed into the air or environment. Spores are collected from mature mushrooms and can be used for propagation. However, spore inoculation requires specific techniques and expertise. It is a more advanced method of cultivation, as it involves germinating spores into mycelium.

2. Mycelium on Grain: Mycelium on grain spawn is one of the most commonly used forms of spawn. It involves growing mycelium on a nutrient-rich substrate such as grains (e.g., rye, wheat, millet). The mycelium colonizes the grains, creating a network of white threads. Mycelium on grain spawn is widely available commercially and offers convenience and ease of use for cultivators. It is typically used for species such as oyster mushrooms, shiitake, and lion's mane.

3. Mycelium on Other Substrates: Some mushrooms require specialized substrates for their mycelium to grow and colonize. In these cases, spawn can be found on alternative substrates such as sterilized wood chips, sawdust, or even liquid culture. The mycelium is allowed to grow on the specific substrate, which will later serve as the inoculum for cultivation. For example, oyster mushrooms can be found on a substrate of grain spawn or sawdust spawn.

Understanding the type of spawn to use depends on factors such as the mushroom species being cultivated, availability, ease of handling, and the cultivator's level of expertise. Each type of spawn has its advantages and considerations.

Spores offer a cost-effective means of propagating mushrooms but require specialized techniques for germination. They are suitable for experienced cultivators who have mastered the necessary methods.

Mycelium on grain spawn is widely used due to its availability, reliability, and ease of handling. It offers a ready-to-use inoculum for many common mushroom species, making it accessible to beginners and experienced cultivators alike.

Mycelium on other substrates, such as wood chips or sawdust, caters to specific mushroom species with unique substrate requirements. These spawn types require more expertise in preparation and handling but offer opportunities for cultivating a diverse range of mushrooms.

When choosing spawn, it is important to consider factors such as the mushroom species you intend to cultivate, your level of experience, availability, and the specific cultivation methods you are employing. Be sure to source spawn from reputable suppliers known for their quality and reliability.

Purchasing and Handling Spawn

Purchasing high-quality spawns is essential for successful mushroom cultivation. Proper handling of spawns is equally important to ensure their viability and prevent contamination. Here are some guidelines for purchasing and handling spawn effectively:

1. Supplier Reputation: Choose a reputable supplier known for producing reliable and high-quality spawns. Look for suppliers with a good track record, positive reviews, and certifications for spawn production. Seek recommendations from experienced cultivators or join online communities dedicated to mushroom cultivation to gather insights on reputable suppliers.

2. Freshness: Spawn should be fresh to ensure its viability. Check the manufacturing or packaging date to ensure you are purchasing the most recent batch. Fresh spawn has a higher chance of successful colonization and mushroom fruiting. Avoid purchasing spawn that is close to or past its expiration date.

3. Storage Conditions: Spawns should be stored in appropriate conditions to maintain their viability. Follow the supplier's instructions for storage temperature and duration. Improper storage can lead to reduced viability and poor performance of the spawn. Most spawns should be stored in a cool, dark place to prolong their shelf life.

4. Hygiene and Sterility: Maintain a clean and sterile environment when handling spawn. Contamination can hinder mycelium growth and lead to poor mushroom development. Use

gloves, masks, and sanitized tools to minimize the risk of contamination. Avoid touching the spawn directly with bare hands to prevent introducing contaminants.

5. Quantity: Determine the quantity of spawn you need based on the size of your cultivation project. It is recommended to purchase slightly more spawn than required to account for any potential losses or additional inoculations. Having extra spawn on hand allows for flexibility in case of unforeseen circumstances.

6. Labeling: Keep track of the spawn's origin, batch number, and any specific instructions provided by the supplier. Proper labeling will help you organize and maintain accurate records throughout the cultivation process. This information can be valuable for troubleshooting, tracking performance, and future reference.

7. Handling Techniques: When handling spawn, it is crucial to prevent physical damage or excessive agitation. Rough handling can disrupt the delicate mycelium and reduce its ability to colonize the substrate effectively. Carefully open spawn containers or bags, ensuring minimal disturbance to the mycelium. Avoid exposing spawns to excessive heat or direct sunlight, as it can negatively impact their viability.

8. Timely Inoculation: Inoculate the substrate with the spawn as soon as possible after receiving it. Delaying inoculation can lead to a decline in viability and an increased risk of contamination. Plan your cultivation process to ensure timely inoculation once all the necessary preparations are complete.

PREPARING THE SUBSTRATE

The substrate is the material on which mushrooms grow. Understanding different types of substrates and their preparation methods is essential for creating an optimal environment for mycelium colonization and mushroom development.

Understanding Substrate

Substrates provide the necessary nutrients, structure, and moisture for mushroom growth. Common substrates include straw, wood chips, sawdust, agricultural waste, and various combinations of these materials. Different mushrooms have specific substrate requirements, so it is important to choose the appropriate substrate for your chosen mushroom species.

- Straw: Straw is a widely used substrate for cultivating mushrooms such as oyster mushrooms. It is readily available and affordable and provides a favorable environment for mycelium colonization. Wheat straw and oat straw are commonly used, and the substrate is typically pasteurized to kill off competing organisms before inoculation.
- Wood Chips: Wood-based substrates are suitable for mushrooms like shiitake and lion's mane. Hardwood chips, such as oak or beech, are preferred. Wood chips need to be properly prepared through a process called "sterilization" or "pasteurization" to eliminate competing organisms and make the substrate more receptive to mycelium colonization.

- Sawdust: Sawdust is a fine material obtained from wood processing. It is commonly used for cultivating mushrooms such as shiitake, oyster mushrooms, and lion's mane. Sawdust substrates need to be sterilized to remove any contaminants and create a favorable environment for mycelium growth.
- Agricultural Waste: Various agricultural waste materials can serve as substrates, such as corn cobs, cottonseed hulls, coffee grounds, or straws supplemented with manure. These substrates are often used for mushrooms like wine caps and oyster mushrooms. Proper preparation, including pasteurization or sterilization, is necessary to remove competing organisms.
- Combinations: Some mushrooms benefit from a combination of substrates. For example, a mixture of straw and sawdust can provide an ideal substrate for oyster mushrooms.

Preparing Different Substrates

Preparing substrates involves proper treatment to create a favorable environment for mycelium colonization and inhibit the growth of competing organisms. The specific preparation method will depend on the substrate and the mushroom species. Here are general steps for preparing different substrates:

1. Collect and Prepare the Substrate Material: Obtain the desired substrate material, such as straw, wood chips, or sawdust. Remove any contaminants, such as rocks or foreign objects. Cut or chop the materials into suitable sizes, if necessary, to facilitate proper colonization and moisture retention.

2. Soaking or Wetting: Some substrates, such as straw, may require soaking in water to increase their moisture content. Soaking can also aid in breaking down complex carbohydrates and making the substrate more accessible to mycelium colonization. For other substrates like wood chips or sawdust, wetting or hydrating the material is sufficient to achieve the desired moisture level.

3. Pasteurization or Sterilization: To eliminate competing organisms and create a sterile environment, pasteurization or sterilization is necessary. Pasteurization involves heating

the substrate to a specific temperature range (usually around 140-160°F or 60-70°C) for a set duration. This process kills off most contaminants while allowing beneficial microorganisms to survive. Sterilization involves subjecting the substrate to higher temperatures (around 250°F or 121°C) under pressure, eliminating both beneficial and harmful microorganisms. The method chosen will depend on the substrate and the mushroom species you are cultivating.

4. Cooling and Draining: After pasteurization or sterilization, the substrate needs to cool down to room temperature. Excess moisture should be drained to achieve the desired moisture content for the specific mushroom species. Proper moisture levels are critical for mycelium growth and development.

5. Adjusting pH: Some mushrooms have specific pH preferences for optimal growth. Measure the pH of the substrate and make adjustments if necessary, using suitable amendments such as hydrated lime or gypsum. Follow recommended guidelines or consult experts to ensure the substrate pH aligns with the mushroom species' preferences.

6. Conditioning and Aging (Optional): For certain substrates like straw, a conditioning or aging process may be beneficial. This involves subjecting the substrate to a controlled decomposition phase to enhance its nutritional value and create a more favorable environment for mycelium colonization.

Properly preparing substrates ensures they are nutritionally balanced, free from contaminants, and receptive to mycelium colonization. Following the appropriate substrate preparation techniques for the specific mushroom species you are cultivating will increase the chances of successful colonization and subsequent mushroom fruiting.

Let's delve into more detail on preparing different substrates for mushroom cultivation:

1. Straw:

1. Collect and prepare the straw by removing any debris or foreign objects. Cut or chop the straw into suitable lengths if necessary.

2. Soak the straw in water for a period of time, typically 12-24 hours, to increase its moisture content and soften the straw fibers.

3. Drain the excess water from the soaked straw to achieve the desired moisture level. Squeezing or pressing the straw can help remove excess water.

4. Pasteurize the straw by heating it to a specific temperature range of around 140-160°F (60-70°C) for a certain duration, typically 1-2 hours. This process helps eliminate competing organisms while preserving beneficial microorganisms.

2. Wood Chips:

1. Collect hardwood chips, preferably from species such as oak or beech. Avoid wood chips from treated or contaminated sources.

2. Prepare the wood chips by removing any foreign objects or large pieces that may hinder colonization.
3. Wet the wood chips by spraying or soaking them in water. Ensure the chips are evenly moistened without excessive waterlogging.
4. Sterilize the wood chips by subjecting them to higher temperatures, around 250°F (121°C), under pressure for a certain period. Sterilization helps eliminate both beneficial and harmful microorganisms, creating a sterile environment for colonization.

3. Sawdust:

1. Obtain hardwood or a mixture of hardwood and softwood sawdust from reliable sources. Ensure the sawdust is clean and free from contaminants.
2. Moisturize the sawdust by adding water and thoroughly mixing it until the moisture is evenly distributed. The sawdust should have a damp texture without being overly wet.
3. Sterilize the sawdust by subjecting it to higher temperatures, around 250°F (121°C), under pressure for a specific duration. Sterilization eliminates competing organisms, allowing for successful mycelium colonization.

4. Agricultural Waste:

1. Collect the desired agricultural waste material such as corn cobs, cottonseed hulls, coffee grounds, or straw supplemented with manure.
2. Remove any contaminants or foreign objects from the agricultural waste material.
3. Depending on the specific waste material, soaking or wetting may be necessary to achieve the desired moisture content.
4. Pasteurize or sterilize the agricultural waste substrate based on its composition and the requirements of the mushroom species you are cultivating.

Remember to cool the substrates after pasteurization or sterilization to room temperature before inoculation with spawn or mycelium. Adjust the pH of the substrate if needed to match the preferences of the mushroom species.

INOCULATING THE SUBSTRATE

Inoculation is the process of introducing mushroom spawn or mycelium into the prepared substrate. It is a critical step that establishes the foundation for mycelium colonization and subsequent mushroom development.

Inoculation Process

The inoculation process is a critical step in mushroom cultivation where the spawn or mycelium is introduced into the prepared substrate. This step sets the stage for mycelium colonization and eventual mushroom growth. Understanding the inoculation process is essential for successful cultivation. Let's explore the details of the inoculation process.

1. Sterile Environment: Maintaining a sterile environment is crucial during inoculation to minimize the risk of contamination. Work in a clean and sanitized area, ideally in a laminar flow hood or a still-air box. Wear gloves, a mask, and a clean lab coat or sterile clothing to reduce the introduction of contaminants.

2. Preparation of Spawn: Depending on the type of spawn you are using, there are specific steps to prepare it for inoculation:

   - Spore Inoculation: If using spores, they need to be germinated into a mycelium. This involves creating a suitable environment for spore germination, such as a petri dish or agar plate containing a nutrient-rich agar medium. The spores are dispersed onto the agar surface and allowed to germinate into mycelium under controlled conditions. Once the mycelium has grown sufficiently, small pieces of the agar with mycelium (called agar wedges or agar plugs) are used for inoculation.

   - Grain Spawn: Grain spawn usually comes in jars or bags. Prior to inoculation, shake the grain spawn container to distribute the mycelium evenly throughout the grains. If using larger grain spawn, break it up into smaller pieces or crush it slightly to increase the contact area with the substrate.

   - Mycelium on Other Substrates: If using mycelium grown on other substrates such as wood chips or sawdust, break apart the substrate into smaller pieces or cut slits in the bag to expose the mycelium. This will help create contact points with the substrate during inoculation.

3. Mixing or Layering: Once the spawn is prepared, it needs to be mixed or layered with the substrate:

   - Mixing: In a clean container or cultivation bag, combine the prepared spawn and substrate. Mix thoroughly to distribute the spawn evenly throughout the substrate. This ensures that the mycelium has ample contact with the substrate, facilitating colonization.

- Layering: Alternatively, you can layer the spawn and substrate in the cultivation container or bag. Begin by adding a layer of substrate, followed by a layer of spawn. Repeat this process until all the substrate and spawn are used. Layering provides contact points for the mycelium to spread from the spawn to the surrounding substrate.

4. Incubation: After inoculation, the inoculated substrate needs to be placed in a suitable environment for mycelium colonization. Maintain the proper temperature and humidity conditions specific to the mushroom species you are cultivating. This encourages the mycelium to grow and spread throughout the substrate. It is essential to ensure adequate air exchange and proper ventilation during incubation.

5. Monitoring Colonization: Regularly monitor the progress of mycelium colonization. The mycelium will appear as white, thread-like growth spreading throughout the substrate. Observe the colonization rate and identify any areas that may be slower or show signs of contamination. Maintain records of colonization rates to track progress and identify any issues that may arise.

6. Adjusting Conditions: If necessary, adjust the temperature, humidity, or airflow to promote optimal mycelium growth. Certain mushrooms may require specific conditions for colonization. Consult cultivation guides, experts, or online resources for recommendations tailored to the mushroom species you are cultivating.

Caring for Inoculated Substrate

Caring for the inoculated substrate is crucial to ensure optimal conditions for mycelium growth and colonization. By providing the right environment and maintaining proper care, you can support the development of a robust mycelial network, which is essential for successful mushroom cultivation. Here are key considerations for caring for the inoculated substrate:

1. Temperature: Maintain the appropriate temperature for the specific mushroom species you are cultivating. Different mushrooms have different temperature preferences for optimal mycelium growth. Generally, maintaining a temperature between 70°F to 80°F (21°C to 27°C) promotes vigorous mycelial growth for many common mushroom species. Use a thermometer to monitor and adjust the temperature if needed.

2. Humidity: Adequate humidity is vital to support mycelium growth and prevent drying out. Maintain a consistent level of humidity to provide a moist environment for the mycelium. The desired humidity range depends on the mushroom species and can typically range from 80% to 95%. Use a hygrometer or humidity gauge to monitor and adjust the humidity level as necessary. Mist the growing area or use a humidifier to increase humidity when needed.

3. Air Exchange: Proper air exchange is crucial for providing fresh oxygen and removing carbon dioxide. Mycelium requires oxygen for respiration, and stagnant air can impede growth. Ensure adequate airflow around the inoculated substrate by creating ventilation holes or using air filters. Strike a balance between fresh air exchange and minimizing the risk of contamination.

4. Light Exposure: Most mushrooms do not require direct exposure to light during the colonization phase. Keep the inoculated substrate in a relatively dark environment. However, some mushrooms, such as those in the genus Psilocybe, may benefit from indirect light or specific light cycles. Research the light requirements of the mushroom species you are cultivating and provide the appropriate lighting conditions if necessary.

5. Contamination Prevention: Maintain a clean and sterile environment to minimize the risk of contamination. Practice good hygiene by wearing gloves, a mask, and a clean lab coat or sterile clothing when handling the inoculated substrate. Regularly clean and sanitize the cultivation area and equipment. Keep potential sources of contamination, such as pests, mold, and bacteria, away from the growing area.

6. Monitoring and Troubleshooting: Regularly monitor the progress of mycelium growth and colonization. Observe the appearance and rate of mycelial growth, ensuring it spreads uniformly throughout the substrate. Look out for any signs of contamination, such as off-color growth, foul odors, or unusual textures. If contamination occurs, take immediate action to address the issue and prevent its spread. Maintain detailed records of observations and any adjustments made to track progress and troubleshoot any issues that arise.

7. Patience and Observation: Mycelium growth takes time, and it's important to be patient during the colonization phase. The speed of colonization varies depending on the mushroom species, substrate composition, temperature, and other environmental factors. Regularly check the substrate for progress, but avoid excessive disturbance that may disrupt the mycelial network.

By carefully monitoring and providing proper care for the inoculated substrate, you create optimal conditions for mycelium growth and colonization. This stage is crucial for establishing a strong foundation that will eventually lead to the formation of mushrooms. As the mycelium spreads and strengthens, it prepares the substrate for the exciting next phase—the fruiting stage, where mushrooms begin to develop.

PART 2

Chapter 4

THE GROWTH CYCLE AND HARVESTING

FROM MYCELIUM TO FRUITING

The growth cycle of mushrooms, from mycelium to fruiting, is a fascinating journey that unfolds in several distinct stages. It all begins with the mycelium, a network of thread-like structures that serve as the vegetative part of the fungus. The mycelium spreads and infiltrates a substrate, which can be a variety of materials such as compost, wood chips, or straw.

During the colonization stage, the mycelium establishes itself within the substrate, breaking down complex organic matter and absorbing nutrients. This process can take several weeks or even months, depending on the mushroom species and environmental conditions. The mycelium continues to grow and expand, creating a robust network throughout the substrate.

As the mycelium matures, it enters a phase known as primordia formation. Primordia are tiny, pin-like structures that appear on the surface of the substrate. These primordia represent the initial stages of mushroom development and indicate that fruiting is about to occur.

Under the right environmental conditions, which include appropriate temperature, humidity, and light, the primordia grow and differentiate into recognizable mushroom structures. The mycelium directs its energy towards the development of these fruiting bodies, which typically emerge from the substrate and begin to enlarge.

As the mushrooms mature, they undergo significant changes in appearance, size, and color. The cap expands, the stem elongates, and the gills or pores on the underside of the cap develop. This growth process can take several days or weeks, depending on the species.

Once the mushrooms have reached their full maturity, they are ready for harvesting. Careful attention is given to the timing of the harvest, as it directly impacts the flavor, texture, and overall quality of the mushrooms. Harvesting involves gently twisting or cutting the mature mushrooms at the base of the stem, being careful not to disturb the surrounding mycelium.

After harvesting, the mycelium and remaining substrate can be left to regenerate, potentially producing additional flushes of mushrooms. Alternatively, the spent substrate can be recycled or composted for other purposes.

Understanding Mycelium Growth

Understanding mycelium growth is essential for anyone interested in cultivating mushrooms or studying fungal biology. Mycelium refers to the branching network of thread-like structures called hyphae that make up the vegetative part of fungi. Here's a breakdown of the key aspects of mycelium growth:

1. Germination

The growth cycle begins with the germination of spores or mycelial fragments. These microscopic reproductive units serve as the starting point for mycelium formation. When conditions are favorable, such as suitable temperature, moisture, and nutrient availability, spores or mycelial fragments initiate the germination process.

2. Hyphal Expansion

Once germination occurs, hyphae begin to extend and branch out. Hyphae are cylindrical, filamentous structures that elongate at their tips. They are composed of a tubular cell wall containing cytoplasm, which contains the various organelles necessary for growth and metabolism. Hyphae secrete enzymes to break down organic matter in their surroundings, allowing them to absorb nutrients.

3. Colonization

As the hyphae grow, they explore the surrounding environment, colonizing and spreading through the substrate. This colonization process is crucial for acquiring nutrients and establishing a network that facilitates resource uptake. The mycelium may exhibit a radial or linear growth pattern, depending on the species and substrate conditions.

4. Nutrient Absorption

The mycelium secretes enzymes, such as cellulases or ligninases, which help break down complex organic compounds present in the substrate. These enzymes break down large molecules into smaller, soluble forms that can be easily absorbed by the mycelium. This nutrient absorption sustains the growth and expansion of the mycelial network.

5. Mycelial Fusion

In some cases, neighboring mycelial strands from the same or different individuals can come into contact and fuse together. This process, known as anastomosis, results in the formation of a network with interconnected hyphae. Mycelial fusion enhances resource sharing and genetic exchange between fungal individuals.

6. Environmental Influence

Mycelium growth is influenced by various environmental factors. Temperature, humidity, light, pH levels, and nutrient availability play crucial roles in determining the rate and quality of mycelial growth. Different mushroom species have specific environmental preferences, and optimizing these conditions is essential for successful cultivation.

Recognizing and Encouraging Fruiting

Recognizing and encouraging fruiting in mushroom cultivation is a crucial step in the process of obtaining a bountiful harvest. Here are some key points to consider when it comes to recognizing and encouraging fruiting:

1. Environmental Conditions

Mushrooms have specific requirements for temperature, humidity, light, and fresh air exchange to initiate fruiting. Understanding the optimal conditions for the particular mushroom species you are growing is essential. Adjusting these environmental factors to mimic the natural habitat of the mushrooms can help stimulate fruiting.

2. Temperature

Different mushroom species have different temperature preferences for fruiting. Some require cooler temperatures, while others thrive in warmer conditions. Monitoring and maintaining the appropriate temperature range during the fruiting stage is crucial. A slight drop in temperature can sometimes trigger the formation of primordia (baby mushrooms) and initiate fruiting.

3. Humidity

Mushrooms thrive in high humidity environments, as it helps prevent drying out and promotes proper development. Maintaining a consistent humidity level, typically around 85-95%, can be achieved through misting or by using humidifiers. Be careful not to oversaturate the growing environment, as excess moisture can lead to issues like mold or bacterial contamination.

4. Light

Light plays a vital role in triggering and directing mushroom fruiting. While different mushroom species have varying light requirements, most benefit from a combination of natural and artificial light. Providing indirect light or exposure to low-intensity fluorescent or LED lighting for a few hours a day can simulate daylight conditions and stimulate fruiting.

5. Fresh Air Exchange

Mushrooms require proper air circulation for successful fruiting. Carbon dioxide buildup can inhibit fruiting, so ensuring adequate fresh air exchange is important. You can achieve this by periodically opening the cultivation area or using fans to circulate air gently. However, avoid direct drafts that may cause fluctuations in temperature or humidity.

6. Primordia Formation

Primordia are the early stages of mushroom development, appearing as small pinheads or bumps on the substrate. Recognizing the formation of primordia is a sign that fruiting is imminent. Once primordia appear, it is important to maintain stable environmental conditions to support their growth into mature mushrooms.

7. Harvesting and Maintenance

Harvesting mature mushrooms in a timely manner encourages further fruiting. Carefully pluck or cut the mushrooms at the base of the stem, being mindful not to disturb the mycelium. Proper maintenance of the growing environment, including regular misting, humidity control, and adjusting temperature and light as needed, will help promote subsequent flushes of mushrooms.

HARVESTING YOUR MUSHROOMS

Harvesting your mushrooms is an exciting and rewarding step in the cultivation process. It is the culmination of your efforts and patience as you get to enjoy the delicious and nutritious fruits of your labor. Proper harvesting techniques ensure that you gather the mushrooms at the right time and in the correct manner, maximizing their flavor, texture, and overall quality. In this guide, we will explore the essential aspects of harvesting mushrooms, providing you with valuable insights to ensure a successful and enjoyable harvest.

When to Harvest

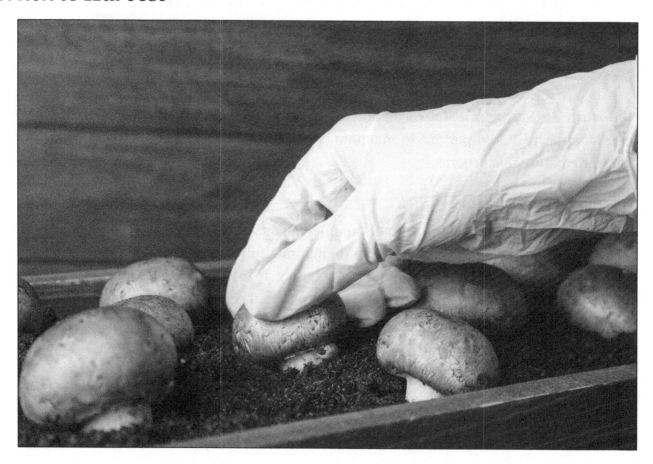

Knowing when to harvest your mushrooms is crucial for obtaining the best flavor, texture, and overall quality. The timing of the harvest depends on the specific mushroom species you are cultivating, as each species has its own growth patterns and maturation stages. Here are some general guidelines to help you determine the ideal time to harvest your mushrooms:

1. Observe the Mushroom Growth

Regularly monitor the growth of your mushrooms. As they develop, you will notice changes in their appearance and size. Young mushrooms start as small pinheads or bumps on the substrate, and they gradually grow larger and take on their characteristic shape. Observe how the caps expand, the gills or pores develop, and the stems elongate or thicken. This visual observation will help you track the progress and maturity of your mushrooms.

2. Check for Veil Break

In some mushroom species, a thin membrane called the veil covers the gills or pore surface when the mushroom is young. As the mushroom matures, the veil naturally breaks, exposing the gills or pores. The veil break is an indication that the mushroom is approaching its prime for harvesting. It is best to harvest the mushrooms shortly after the veil break, ensuring optimal flavor and texture.

3. Consider Cap Opening

Pay attention to the cap opening of your mushrooms. Some species have caps that initially appear rounded or convex but gradually flatten or even become concave as they mature. When the caps are fully opened or flattened, it suggests that the mushrooms are at their peak for harvesting. However, be cautious not to wait too long, as overly mature mushrooms may release spores, which can affect their taste and texture.

4. Spore Development

Spore development is another factor to consider when determining the harvest time. As mushrooms mature, they produce and release spores. While spore release is a natural part of the mushroom's life cycle, excessive spore production can negatively impact the flavor and appearance of the mushrooms. It is generally recommended to harvest mushrooms before they release a significant number of spores. Harvesting at this stage ensures a more enjoyable culinary experience.

5. Taste Testing

When you are growing mushrooms for personal consumption, taste testing can be an effective way to determine the harvest time. As the mushrooms reach their potential maturity, try sampling a small portion to assess their flavor and texture. This subjective evaluation can guide you in deciding whether the mushrooms are ready for harvest or if they need a little more time to develop.

6. Reference Cultivation Guides

Consulting cultivation guides or resources specific to the mushroom species you are growing is highly beneficial. These guides often provide detailed information on the average time to harvest for different mushroom varieties, as well as specific visual indicators to look for during the maturation process. Understanding the unique characteristics of your chosen mushroom species will help you make informed decisions regarding the optimal harvest time.

How to Harvest

Harvesting mushrooms requires careful handling and proper techniques to ensure the preservation of quality and to avoid damaging the mushrooms or the mycelium. Here's a step-by-step guide on how to harvest your mushrooms effectively:

1. Gather Your Tools

Before you begin the harvest, gather the necessary tools and materials. You will need clean gloves or washed hands, a sharp knife or scissors, a clean container or basket, and a soft brush or paper towel for cleaning if needed.

2. Hygiene Precautions

Maintain proper hygiene during the harvest process to minimize the risk of contamination. Wear clean gloves or wash your hands thoroughly to prevent the transfer of contaminants to the mushrooms. Sterilize your cutting tool by wiping it with rubbing alcohol or dipping it in a diluted bleach solution and then rinsing it with clean water. This helps reduce the risk of introducing unwanted microorganisms to the mushrooms.

3. Harvesting Technique

When it comes to harvesting mushrooms, a gentle and precise technique is essential to avoid damaging the mushrooms or the mycelium. Follow these steps:

4. Hold the Base

Firmly hold the base of the mushroom stem between your thumb and forefinger. Take care not to put excessive pressure on the cap or twist the mushroom, as this can cause damage.

5. Make a Clean Cut

Using a sharp knife or scissors, make a clean and precise cut just above the surface of the substrate or at the point where the stem meets the substrate. Ensure that the cut is smooth and even to minimize the risk of introducing contaminants or damaging the remaining mycelium.

6. Repeat the Process

Continue harvesting each mushroom individually, taking care to maintain the cleanliness of your tools and hands between each cut. Harvest mature mushrooms while leaving smaller, undeveloped ones to grow further for subsequent harvests.

7. Handle with Care

Handle the harvested mushrooms with care to avoid bruising or damaging them. Place them gently into a clean container or basket, taking care not to overcrowd or stack them on top of each other. Rough handling can lead to bruising, which affects the appearance and quality of the mushrooms.

8. Cleaning, if Necessary

If the mushrooms have debris or substrate stuck to them, you can lightly clean them. Use a soft brush or a paper towel to brush off any dirt or debris. Avoid washing the mushrooms unless absolutely necessary, as they are highly absorbent and can become waterlogged, affecting their texture and flavor.

9. Post-Harvest Handling

After harvesting, it is crucial to handle the mushrooms properly to maintain their freshness and quality. If you plan to consume them immediately, keep them in a breathable container, such as a paper bag or a container with ventilation holes, to maintain airflow. Store them in the refrigerator, preferably in the crisper drawer, to extend their shelf life.

10. Storing Excess Harvest

If you have harvested more mushrooms than you can consume right away, there are several methods to preserve them. Drying mushrooms is a popular preservation technique that concentrates their flavor and allows for long-term storage. Freezing or canning mushrooms are also options depending on your preference and the mushroom variety. Remember to follow specific preservation guidelines for each method to ensure the best results.

Chapter 5

POST-HARVEST PROCESSING AND STORAGE

CLEANING AND PROCESSING

Post-harvest processing and proper storage are crucial steps to maintain the quality, freshness, and longevity of harvested mushrooms.

Cleaning Techniques

Cleaning mushrooms properly is crucial to remove any dirt, debris, or potential contaminants while preserving their delicate texture and flavor. Proper cleaning ensures that the mushrooms are safe to consume and enhances their visual appeal. Before cleaning, carefully inspect the mushrooms for any visible signs of spoilage or damage. Look for discoloration, slime, or an unpleasant odor. Sorting out damaged mushrooms ensures that only fresh and healthy ones are cleaned and used. Here is a comprehensive guide on cleaning techniques for mushrooms:

Dry Cleaning Method:

1. Gently brush off any visible dirt or debris from the mushrooms using a soft-bristled brush or a mushroom brush. Start from the stem and brush towards the cap to remove any loose particles. The brush should have soft bristles to avoid damaging the mushroom's delicate surface.
2. Alternatively, a clean, dry cloth can be used to wipe away dirt. Gently rub the mushroom's surface to remove any dirt or debris. Be careful not to press too hard, as this can bruise or damage the mushroom.

Wet cleaning method:

1. Rinse under cold water:

- For sturdier mushrooms like cremini, button, or portobello, rinse them quickly under cold running water. Hold the mushroom by the stem or cap and gently rub off any dirt or debris using your fingertips. Use a gentle rubbing motion to avoid damaging the mushroom's surface. Avoid soaking the mushrooms as they tend to absorb water, which can affect their texture and flavor.

2. Soaking:

- Some mushrooms with denser caps, such as morels or shiitakes, benefit from a gentle soak to remove dirt. Fill a bowl with cold water and place the mushrooms in it. Allow them to soak for a few minutes to loosen any dirt. Gently swirl them with your hand to dislodge any remaining debris. Avoid extended soaking to prevent water absorption, which can affect the mushroom's texture.

3. Draining:

- After rinsing or soaking, drain the mushrooms thoroughly. Gently shake off excess water and place them on a clean towel or paper towel in a single layer. Avoid stacking or overcrowding the mushrooms, as this can lead to moisture buildup and potential spoilage.

Pat drying:

1. Gently pat dry the mushrooms using a clean kitchen towel or paper towel. Carefully blot the mushrooms to absorb any remaining moisture. Be gentle to avoid damaging the mushrooms' delicate structure. Ensure the mushrooms are completely dry before further processing or storage.

Trim and discard:

2. Inspect the mushrooms again after cleaning and drying. Trim any discolored or damaged parts using a sharp knife. Remove any tough or woody stems, if applicable, as they may not be pleasant to eat. Discard the trimmings and any undesirable parts.

Optional: Additional cleaning for certain mushroom varieties:

1. Morels:

- Morels often have crevices where dirt and debris can accumulate. Slice the morels lengthwise to expose the inner parts and inspect for any hidden debris. Rinse gently under cold water or use a soft brush to clean out any remaining dirt. Avoid excessive water exposure, as morels are porous and can absorb water easily.

2. Maitake and Hen of the Woods:

- These mushrooms have dense, layered structures. Use a soft brush or a damp cloth to remove any visible dirt or debris. Gently brush or wipe the surface, paying attention to the folds and crevices. Avoid prolonged water exposure, as they can become waterlogged.

Once the mushrooms are cleaned, dried, and trimmed, inspect them one last time to ensure they are clean and ready for use. Look for any remaining dirt or blemishes and clean as needed.

It's important to note that mushrooms have different cleaning requirements depending on their variety, so always refer to specific cleaning recommendations for the particular mushroom species you are working with.

Processing for Consumption or Sale

Processing mushrooms involves various techniques to prepare them for consumption or sale while preserving their quality, enhancing their flavor, and extending their shelf life. Proper processing ensures that mushrooms are safe to consume and appealing to customers. Here is a comprehensive guide on processing mushrooms:

1. Cleaning:

- Assess the mushrooms: Before processing, carefully inspect the mushrooms for any visible signs of spoilage or damage. Sort out damaged or spoiled mushrooms and discard them.

- Dry cleaning method: Gently brush off any visible dirt or debris from the mushrooms using a soft-bristled brush or a mushroom brush. Start from the stem and brush towards the cap to remove loose particles. Alternatively, use a clean, dry cloth to wipe away dirt from the mushroom's surface.
- Wet cleaning method: Rinse the mushrooms briefly under cold running water. Gently rub off any dirt or debris using your fingertips. Avoid soaking the mushrooms to prevent water absorption, which can affect their texture and flavor. For mushrooms with denser caps, like morels or shiitakes, a gentle soak in cold water can help remove dirt. Swirl them in a bowl of water and dislodge any remaining debris. Avoid extended soaking to prevent water absorption.

2. Trimming:

- After cleaning, inspect the mushrooms again and trim any discolored, damaged, or tough parts. Use a sharp knife to remove these portions. Discard the trimmings.
- Remove tough or woody stems, if applicable, as they may not be pleasant to eat. Trim the stems neatly for a visually appealing appearance.

3. Slicing or Dicing:

- Depending on the desired application and market demand, mushrooms can be sliced or diced. Use a sharp knife to cut them into even slices or cubes, maintaining a consistent thickness for uniform cooking or presentation.
- For larger mushrooms, consider quartering or halving them to achieve the desired size.

4. Blanching (optional):

- Blanching is a brief boiling process that helps preserve the mushrooms' color, texture, and shelf life. It also helps kill any surface bacteria.
- Bring a pot of water to a boil and add the mushrooms. Blanch them for a short period (around 1-2 minutes) and then immediately transfer them to an ice bath to stop the cooking process. Drain well before further processing.

5. Cooking or Preserving:

- Mushrooms can be cooked using various methods such as sautéing, grilling, baking, or incorporating them into soups, stews, or sauces. Follow specific recipes and techniques for desired dishes.
- For preserving mushrooms, methods include drying, canning, pickling, or fermenting. Each preservation method requires specific equipment and techniques, so follow established recipes or guidelines.

6. Packaging and Storage:

- Package the processed mushrooms in appropriate containers or packaging materials. Use airtight containers or vacuum-sealed bags to maintain freshness and prevent moisture loss. Label the packaging with essential information such as the mushroom variety, date of processing, and any special instructions.
- Store processed mushrooms in a cool, dry place away from direct sunlight. Proper storage conditions will depend on the specific processing method and product. Follow recommended guidelines or consult experts for specific storage requirements.

7. Quality Control and Safety:

- Implement quality control measures to ensure the processed mushrooms meet high standards. Regularly inspect the products for any signs of spoilage, mold, or off-flavors. Establish protocols to remove any defective products.
- Adhere to food safety guidelines and regulations. Maintain a clean processing area, practice good hygiene, and follow proper sanitation procedures. Implement temperature controls and monitor for any signs of contamination or deterioration.

8. Labeling and Certification:

- If processing mushrooms for sale, ensure compliance with labeling regulations. Include necessary information such as product name, ingredients, allergen warnings, nutritional facts, and contact information.
- Consider obtaining relevant certifications or licenses, such as organic certification, to provide assurance to customers about the quality and integrity of the processed mushrooms.

By following these comprehensive processing techniques, you can transform raw mushrooms into high-quality products ready for consumption or sale. Proper processing not only enhances their flavor and visual appeal but also ensures their safety and extends their shelf life, maximizing their value and customer satisfaction.

STORING AND PRESERVING MUSHROOMS

Storing and preserving mushrooms properly is essential to maintain their quality, flavor, and texture for extended periods. Here are some methods for storing and preserving mushrooms:

1. Refrigeration

Fresh mushrooms are best stored in the refrigerator to slow down spoilage. Choose a breathable container: Place the mushrooms in a paper bag, a mesh bag, or a container with ventilation holes to allow airflow. Line the bottom of the container with a paper towel or clean cloth to absorb excess moisture. Place the mushrooms in a single layer, avoiding overcrowding to prevent bruising and moisture buildup. Put the container with the mushrooms in the refrigerator's crisper drawer, which offers slightly higher humidity. Maintain a temperature of around 36 to 41°F (2 to 5°C) for optimal storage. Check the mushrooms periodically and remove any that show signs of spoilage, such as mold or sliminess.

2. Drying:

Drying mushrooms is an effective preservation method that concentrates their flavors and allows for long-term storage. Use a soft brush or a paper towel to remove any dirt or debris from the mushrooms. Avoid washing them unless necessary, as excessive moisture can prolong the drying process. Depending on the mushroom variety and your preference, slice the mushrooms into uniform pieces or leave them whole. Pre-drying is optional but can help reduce moisture content. Spread the mushrooms in a single layer on a tray or a wire rack and let them air dry for a few hours. Place the pre-dried mushrooms in a dehydrator and set the temperature between 110 to 135°F (43 to 57°C). Follow the manufacturer's instructions for the specific drying time, as it varies depending on the mushroom variety and thickness. If you don't have a dehydrator, you can use an oven. Place the pre-dried mushrooms on a baking sheet lined with parchment paper and set the oven temperature to the lowest setting. Keep the oven door slightly ajar to allow moisture to escape. Check regularly until the mushrooms are dry and crisp. Once fully dried, store the mushrooms in airtight containers or resealable bags. Keep them in a cool, dark place to maintain their quality. Dried mushrooms can last for several months to a year if stored properly.

3. Freezing

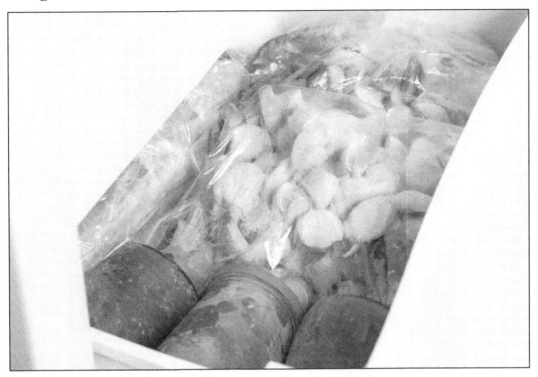

Freezing mushrooms is another option for preserving their texture and flavor. Clean the mushrooms using one of the gentle cleaning methods mentioned earlier. Slice them to your desired thickness. Blanching can help preserve the color, texture, and flavor of mushrooms. Bring a pot of water to a boil, and blanch the sliced mushrooms for 1 to 2 minutes. Transfer them to an ice bath immediately to stop the cooking process. Drain the mushrooms and gently pat them dry with a paper towel to remove excess moisture. Place the sliced or blanched mushrooms in freezer-safe containers or resealable bags. Squeeze out as much air as possible and seal tightly. Label the containers or bags with the date and the contents. Place them in the freezer, keeping the temperature at or below 0°F (-18°C). When you need to use frozen mushrooms, thaw them in the refrigerator before cooking. Avoid refreezing previously frozen mushrooms.

4. Pickling

Pickling mushrooms is a flavorful preservation method that adds tanginess and extends their shelf life. Clean the mushrooms using one of the gentle cleaning methods described earlier. Slice or leave them whole, depending on your preference. In a saucepan, combine equal parts vinegar and water. Add salt, sugar, and desired spices (such as peppercorns, garlic, or herbs) to the liquid. Bring the mixture to a boil and simmer for a few minutes. Blanch the mushrooms in boiling water for a couple of minutes. Drain and immediately transfer them to an ice bath to cool. Place the blanched mushrooms in sterilized jars, leaving some space at the top. Pour the hot pickling liquid over the mushrooms, covering them completely. Seal the jars tightly and store them in the refrigerator. Allow the mushrooms to marinate for at least a week before consuming for optimal flavor. Pickled mushrooms can be stored in the refrigerator for several weeks.

Short-Term Storage

1. Refrigeration

Refrigeration is the most common method for short-term storage of mushrooms. Transfer the mushrooms to a breathable container: Place the mushrooms in a paper bag, a mesh bag, or a container with ventilation holes. This allows for proper air circulation and helps prevent moisture buildup.

2. Paper Towel Method

Another method for short-term storage is the paper towel method. Place a clean, damp paper towel on a plate or in a container. Gently arrange the mushrooms on top of the damp paper towel. Cover the mushrooms with another damp paper towel. Store the plate or container in the refrigerator. Check regularly and change the paper towels if they become too wet or dirty.

Long-term Preservation Techniques

1. Drying

Drying mushrooms is a popular method for long-term preservation as it removes moisture and concentrates their flavors. Clean the mushrooms using a soft brush or a paper towel to remove any dirt or debris. Avoid washing them unless necessary, as excess moisture can prolong the drying process.

2. Freezing

Freezing mushrooms is another effective method for long-term preservation. Blanching can help preserve the color, texture, and flavor of mushrooms. Bring a pot of water to a boil, and blanch the sliced mushrooms for 1 to 2 minutes. Transfer them to an ice bath immediately to stop the cooking process.

3. Pickling

Pickling mushrooms is a flavorful preservation method that can be enjoyed for an extended period. Prepare the pickling liquid: In a saucepan, combine equal parts vinegar and water. Add salt, sugar, and desired spices (such as peppercorns, garlic, or herbs) to the liquid. Bring the mixture to a boil and simmer for a few minutes.

Chapter 6

TROUBLESHOOTING AND DEALING WITH COMMON ISSUES

RECOGNIZING AND MANAGING DISEASES

Identifying Common Mushroom Diseases

When cultivating mushrooms, it's important to be aware of common issues and diseases that can affect their growth. Here are some common problems and diseases you may encounter, along with troubleshooting tips and prevention measures:

1. Contamination

Contamination occurs when unwanted fungi, bacteria, or mold infiltrates the growing environment. It can lead to poor mushroom growth or even complete crop loss. To address contamination:

- Ensure your growing area is clean and free from potential sources of contamination. Sterilize equipment, surfaces, and containers before use.
- Wash your hands thoroughly before handling mushrooms or working in the growing area.
- Ensure proper pasteurization or sterilization of the substrate to minimize the risk of contamination.
- Maintain appropriate temperature and humidity levels to discourage the growth of contaminants.

2. Mushroom pests

Various pests can impact mushroom cultivation, including mites, flies, and beetles. These pests can damage the mushrooms and reduce yields. To control pests:

- Remove any decaying or infected mushrooms promptly, as they can attract pests.
- Regularly inspect your growing area for signs of pests. Identify the specific pest to implement effective control measures.
- Implement screens or nets to prevent pests from entering the growing area.
- Introduce natural predators or beneficial insects that feed on pests to control their populations.

3. Mushroom blotch

Mushroom blotch is a common fungal disease that causes discolored spots or blotches on the mushroom caps. To manage mushroom blotch:

- Ensure good air circulation to reduce humidity and prevent moisture buildup, as high humidity can promote disease development.
- Overwatering can create a favorable environment for fungal growth. Water the substrate adequately without causing waterlogged conditions.

- Maintain optimal temperature conditions for the specific mushroom variety, as extreme temperature fluctuations can contribute to disease development.
- Promptly remove any mushrooms showing signs of blotch to prevent further spread of the disease.

4. Mushroom rot

Mushroom rot, often caused by bacteria or fungi, leads to the decay of mushrooms. To prevent mushroom rot:

- Harvest mushrooms when they are mature but still firm to avoid overripening and susceptibility to rot.
- Avoid bruising or damaging the mushrooms during harvesting or post-harvest handling, as injuries can provide entry points for rot-causing microorganisms.
- Monitor and control humidity to prevent excessive moisture that can contribute to rotting development.
- Follow appropriate storage techniques, such as refrigeration or drying, to prevent the growth of rot-causing organisms.

5. Mushroom viruses

Mushroom viruses are microscopic infectious agents that can cause deformities, discoloration, or stunted growth. Prevention is key when it comes to viruses:

- Start with high-quality, virus-free spawn from a reputable supplier.
- Maintain cleanliness in the growing area, sterilize equipment, and avoid cross-contamination between batches.
- Promptly remove and destroy any mushrooms showing virus symptoms to prevent the spread of the disease.
- Avoid growing the same mushroom variety continuously in the same area, as this can increase the risk of virus buildup.

It is crucial to consult with experienced mushroom cultivators, plant pathologists, or agricultural extension services for specific recommendations tailored to your mushroom variety and local conditions. They can provide guidance on disease management and suggest appropriate prevention and treatment strategies based on your specific situation.

Regular monitoring of your mushroom crop is essential to catch early signs of diseases or issues. By taking proactive measures and implementing proper prevention and treatment strategies, you can significantly reduce the impact of diseases and maintain healthy and productive mushroom cultivation.

Prevention and Treatment Strategies

1. Prevention Strategies

- Use high-quality spawn sourced from reputable suppliers to reduce the risk of introducing diseases.
- Regularly clean and sanitize equipment, growing surfaces, and containers to minimize the presence of pathogens.
- Wash your hands thoroughly before handling mushrooms or working in the growing area to prevent the spread of contaminants.
- Follow recommended pasteurization or sterilization techniques to eliminate potential pathogens in the substrate.
- Ensure adequate ventilation in the growing area to prevent excessive humidity and reduce the risk of fungal diseases.
- Maintain optimal environmental conditions specific to the mushroom variety to minimize disease susceptibility.
- Promptly remove any mushrooms showing signs of disease and dispose of them properly to prevent disease spread.

2. Treatment Strategies

- In cases of fungal diseases, specific fungicides may be available for treatment. Consult with a plant pathologist or mushroom cultivation expert for appropriate fungicide options and application methods.
- Consider using beneficial microorganisms or biological agents that can help suppress disease-causing pathogens. These can include beneficial bacteria or fungi that compete with or attack the pathogens.
- Modifying temperature, humidity, and airflow within the growing area can help create less favorable conditions for disease development.
- Isolate infected mushrooms or contaminated materials to prevent the spread of diseases to healthy crops. Dispose of them properly to minimize the risk of reinfection.
- Implement a crop rotation plan, avoiding continuous cultivation of the same mushroom species in the same area. This can help break disease cycles and reduce the buildup of pathogens.
- Clean and disinfect equipment, growing containers, and surfaces to eliminate pathogens that may be present and prevent disease transmission.

Remember that a combination of prevention, early detection, and intervention is key to effectively managing pests in mushroom cultivation. Integrated Pest Management (IPM) practices that combine various strategies are highly recommended to maintain a healthy and pest-free crop. Consult with agricultural extension services or mushroom cultivation experts for specific recommendations tailored to your region and the pests you are dealing with.

DEALING WITH PESTS

It is crucial to consult with experienced mushroom cultivators, plant pathologists, or agricultural extension services for specific recommendations tailored to your mushroom variety and local conditions. They can provide guidance on disease management and suggest appropriate prevention and treatment strategies based on your specific situation.

Regular monitoring of your mushroom crop is essential to catch early signs of diseases or issues. By taking proactive measures and implementing proper prevention and treatment strategies, you can significantly reduce the impact of diseases and maintain healthy and productive mushroom cultivation.

Recognizing Common Pests

It is important to regularly inspect your growing area for signs of pests, including the presence of adult insects, larvae, or damage to mushrooms or growing media. Early detection is crucial for effective pest management. Additionally, maintaining a clean and hygienic growing environment, practicing good sanitation, and implementing preventive measures can help reduce the risk of pest infection. Here is a list of some common pests:

1. Mushroom flies (Sciarid flies)

These small, dark-colored flies are common pests in mushroom cultivation. They lay eggs in the growing substrate, and the larvae feed on mycelium, casing layer, and young mushrooms. Adult flies are attracted to moist environments and can be seen hovering around the growing area.

2. Mushroom mites

Mites are tiny arachnids that can infest mushroom crops. They are often found in high-humidity environments. Mites feed on mycelium and mushroom caps, causing damage and stunted growth.

3. Mushroom beetles (Phorid beetles)

These small beetles are attracted to decaying organic matter, such as spent mushroom substrate. They can lay eggs in the growing medium or on the mushrooms themselves. The larvae of mushroom beetles can cause damage by feeding on mycelium and mushrooms.

4. Fungus gnats

Fungus gnats are small, mosquito-like insects that lay eggs in moist soil or growing media. The larvae feed on organic matter and can damage the mycelium and roots of mushrooms. Adult fungus gnats are attracted to moist conditions and can be seen flying around the growing area.

5. Nematodes

Nematodes are microscopic roundworms that can infect mushroom crops. They are typically soil-borne and can cause damage to the mycelium and roots of mushrooms, leading to stunted growth and yield loss.

6. Slugs and snails

Slugs and snails are common garden pests that can also affect mushroom crops. They are attracted to the moisture and organic matter in the growing environment and can feed on mushrooms, causing damage to the caps.

7. Rodents and mammals

Rodents and mammals, such as mice or rats, can be attracted to the food source provided by mushroom crops. They can cause physical damage to mushrooms, substrate, or casing layers and contaminate the growing environment with their droppings.

Environmentally Friendly Pest Management

Implementing environmentally friendly pest management practices in mushroom cultivation helps minimize the use of synthetic chemicals and reduces the impact on the ecosystem. Here are some eco-friendly strategies to manage pests in a sustainable manner:

1. Cultural Practices

- Maintain cleanliness in the growing area by regularly removing decaying mushrooms, organic debris, and spent substrate. This eliminates potential breeding grounds for pests.
- Rotate mushroom varieties or crops in different areas to disrupt pest life cycles and prevent the buildup of pests in one location.
- Dispose of mushroom waste properly to minimize potential pest infestations. Composting can be done in controlled settings to reduce pest attraction.

2. Biological Control

- Introduce beneficial insects such as predatory mites, nematodes, or beetles that naturally prey on pests like flies, mites, or beetles. They can help control pest populations without the use of chemicals.
- Utilize beneficial microorganisms such as Bacillus thuringiensis or other microbial-based products that specifically target pests while being safe for the environment.
- Integrated Pest Management (IPM), Adopts an integrated approach that combines various biological control methods to manage pests effectively. This includes using natural enemies, monitoring pest populations, and implementing preventive measures.

3. Physical Barriers and Traps

- Install fine-mesh netting around the growing area or vents to prevent flying insects from entering and laying eggs.
- Use yellow or blue sticky traps to attract and capture flying pests like flies, fungus gnats, or beetles.
- Employ physical barriers like screens or covers to keep pests out of the growing area.

4. Habitat Modification

- Optimize airflow and ventilation in the growing environment to reduce excess humidity and discourage pest activity.
- Maintain appropriate moisture levels, avoiding waterlogged conditions that attract pests like flies or mites.
- Use proper lighting techniques to discourage flying insects from entering the growing area.

5. Monitoring and Early Detection

- Monitor your growing area consistently for signs of pest activity, including visual observations of adult insects, larvae, or damage to mushrooms or substrate.
- Set up monitoring traps to capture and identify pests, allowing you to take timely action if pest populations exceed acceptable thresholds.

6. Education and Knowledge Sharing

- Keep up-to-date with the latest research and best practices in environmentally friendly pest management for mushroom cultivation.
- Seek guidance from agricultural extension services, mushroom cultivation experts, or local agricultural organizations for advice and assistance in implementing eco-friendly pest management strategies.

By implementing these environmentally friendly pest management strategies, you can maintain a healthy balance in your mushroom cultivation system while minimizing the impact on the environment. Remember, prevention and early intervention are key to successfully managing pests while maintaining sustainable practices.

PART 3

Chapter 7

ADVANCED TECHNIQUES AND COMMERCIAL CULTIVATION

CULTIVATING EXOTIC AND GOURMET VARIETIES

Choosing Exotic Varieties

When venturing beyond the common button or portobello mushrooms, exploring exotic mushroom varieties can introduce unique flavors, textures, and culinary experiences. Exotic mushrooms offer a wide range of tastes, aromas, and appearances, making them popular among chefs, food enthusiasts, and adventurous home cooks. Here is a comprehensive guide on choosing exotic varieties of mushrooms, including examples of popular options:

1. Research and Familiarize Yourself:

- Start by researching and familiarizing yourself with different exotic mushroom varieties. Learn about their distinct characteristics, flavor profiles, and potential culinary uses. Understanding the unique attributes of each mushroom will help you make informed choices and experiment with diverse flavors in your dishes.

- Explore reputable sources such as books, online resources, and culinary magazines that offer comprehensive information on exotic mushroom varieties. Look for detailed descriptions, cultivation requirements, and suggested cooking methods.

2. Flavor Profiles and Culinary Uses:

- Exotic mushrooms display a wide array of flavors ranging from delicate and nutty to earthy and umami-rich. Consider the flavor profiles that align with your culinary preferences and the dishes you intend to create.

- Assess the culinary uses of different exotic mushrooms. Some varieties are suitable for sautéing, grilling, roasting, or adding to soups and stews, while others are best enjoyed raw in salads or used as garnishes. Understanding the culinary potential of each mushroom will help you select the ones that best complement your desired cooking techniques and recipes.

3. Availability and Freshness:

- Determine the availability of exotic mushrooms in your region. Some varieties may be more readily available in certain seasons or specific geographic areas. Local specialty markets, farmers' markets, and gourmet food stores often carry a range of exotic mushrooms. Consider the availability of fresh and high-quality options to ensure the best culinary experience.

- Examine the freshness of the mushrooms. Look for mushrooms that are firm, plump, and free from blemishes or signs of decay. Mushrooms should have a pleasant aroma without any off odors. Choose mushrooms with intact caps and avoid those with slimy or discolored surfaces.

4. Cultivation Difficulty:

- Consider the cultivation difficulty of different exotic mushroom varieties. Some mushrooms are more challenging to grow and may require specific environmental conditions, specialized techniques, or unique substrates. Evaluate your own cultivation capabilities and determine whether you are willing to invest the time, effort, and resources required to grow certain varieties yourself.

5. Popular Exotic Mushroom Varieties:

Here are examples of popular exotic mushroom varieties, along with their characteristics and culinary uses:

- Morel (Morchella spp.): Morels are highly prized for their unique appearance and complex flavor. They have a honeycomb-like cap and offer a rich, earthy taste. Morels are often sought after for gourmet dishes, including sauces, soups, risottos, and sautés.

- Chanterelle (Cantharellus spp.): Chanterelles are known for their vibrant golden or orange color and delicate, fruity aroma. They possess a mild, slightly peppery flavor with a hint of apricot. Chanterelles are versatile and can be used in various preparations, such as sautés, stir-fries, omelets, and pasta dishes.

- Lion's Mane (Hericium erinaceus): Lion's Mane mushrooms have a distinctive appearance with cascading white tendrils resembling a lion's mane. They offer a seafood-like flavor and a tender, meaty texture. Lion's Mane mushrooms can be pan-fried, roasted, or used in vegetarian and vegan dishes as a meat substitute.
- Maitake (Grifola frondosa): Also known as Hen of the Woods, Maitake mushrooms have a clustered, frilly appearance and a rich, earthy flavor. They are prized for their meaty texture and are often used in stir-fries, soups, and sautés. Maitake mushrooms pair well with Asian-inspired dishes.
- Enoki (Flammulina velutipes): Enoki mushrooms feature long, thin stems and small, delicate caps. They have a mild, slightly sweet flavor and a crunchy texture. Enoki mushrooms are commonly used in salads, soups, hot pots, and stir-fries.
- Shiitake (Lentinula edodes): Shiitake mushrooms are one of the most widely recognized exotic varieties. They have a meaty texture and a robust, umami flavor. Shiitakes are versatile and can be used in a range of dishes, including stir-fries, soups, stews, and even as a meat substitute in vegetarian and vegan recipes.

6. Culinary Pairings:

- Consider the culinary pairings that work well with each exotic mushroom variety. Some mushrooms complement specific ingredients, flavors, or cooking styles. For example, morels pair beautifully with butter, cream, and herbs, while chanterelles often work well with white wine, garlic, and parsley. Understanding the optimal culinary pairings will help you create harmonious and flavorful dishes.

7. Personal Taste and Experimentation:

- Ultimately, choose exotic mushroom varieties based on your personal taste preferences and culinary curiosity. Allow yourself to explore and experiment with different flavors, textures, and cooking techniques. Incorporate exotic mushrooms into your dishes to add depth and intrigue to your culinary creations.

Unique Cultivation Requirements

Exotic mushroom varieties often have specific cultivation requirements that differ from those of common button mushrooms. Understanding these unique needs is crucial to successfully growing and cultivating these specialty mushrooms. Here are some examples of exotic mushroom varieties and their distinctive cultivation requirements:

1. Morel (Morchella spp.):

- Substrate: Morels have unique substrate preferences. They often grow in symbiosis with specific tree species, such as elm, ash, or poplar. Cultivation attempts have involved using a mixture of organic materials like wood chips, sawdust, and peat moss to mimic their natural habitat.

- Temperature and Humidity: Morels typically prefer cool temperatures between 50°F to 60°F (10°C to 15°C) during fruiting. Adequate humidity is crucial to support their growth, usually around 80% to 90% relative humidity.
- Light: Morels generally prefer indirect light or filtered sunlight. Partial shade or dappled light is often recommended for successful fruiting.

2. Chanterelle (Cantharellus spp.):

- Substrate: Chanterelles have a symbiotic relationship with certain tree species, particularly hardwoods like oak, beech, or birch. Cultivation attempts have involved using sterilized wood chips or sawdust supplemented with organic materials like bran or soybean meal.
- Temperature and Humidity: Chanterelles thrive in cooler temperatures ranging from 55°F to 65°F (13°C to 18°C). They prefer humid conditions with around 80% to 90% relative humidity.
- Light: Chanterelles usually prefer indirect or filtered light. They can tolerate slightly more light than some other mushrooms but still benefit from partial shade.

3. Lion's Mane (Hericium erinaceus):

- Substrate: Lion's Mane grows well on hardwood substrates such as logs or sawdust blocks supplemented with nutrients like wheat bran or rice bran. Oak, beech, or maple logs are often used for cultivation.
- Temperature and Humidity: Lion's Mane prefers slightly cooler temperatures ranging from 60°F to 75°F (15°C to 24°C). Adequate humidity levels around 80% to 90% are beneficial for successful growth.
- Light: Lion's Mane typically prefers indirect or filtered light. It can tolerate slightly brighter conditions than some other mushrooms but still benefits from partial shade.

4. Maitake (Grifola frondosa):

- Substrate: Maitake thrives on hardwood substrates such as logs or sawdust blocks. Oak, maple, or beech logs are commonly used for cultivation. Supplementation with nutrient-rich materials like wheat bran or soybean meal can enhance growth.
- Temperature and Humidity: Maitake prefers cooler temperatures ranging from 55°F to 65°F (13°C to 18°C). Higher humidity levels, around 80% to 90%, are favorable for their growth.
- Light: Maitake mushrooms prefer indirect or filtered light. They are typically grown in partially shaded environments.

5. Enoki (Flammulina velutipes):

- Substrate: Enoki mushrooms grow best on sterilized substrates such as wheat straw, supplemented sawdust, or various agricultural waste materials. The substrate should be properly pasteurized or sterilized to prevent contamination.
- Temperature and Humidity: Enoki mushrooms prefer cooler temperatures ranging from 45°F to 60°F (7°C to 15°C). Humidity levels around 85% to 95% are recommended for successful cultivation.
- Light: Enoki mushrooms prefer cool, low-light conditions. They are often grown in cooler environments or refrigeration units to maintain the desired temperature and light conditions.

It's important to note that these are general cultivation requirements for the mentioned exotic mushroom varieties, and specific techniques may vary depending on the cultivator's experience and available resources. Successful cultivation often involves trial and error, as well as a deep understanding of the specific needs and behavior of each mushroom species.

SCALING UP: FROM HOBBY TO BUSINESS

To successfully transition from a mushroom cultivation hobby to a thriving business, it is essential to follow a strategic approach. Here are the key steps to consider:

- **Making a Plan**: Think about your goals. Do you want to sell your mushrooms at a local farmers' market, or supply them to a nearby restaurant? Write down your ideas. This will be your "business plan" - a roadmap for your mushroom-growing adventure.
- **Getting to Know Your Market**: Spend some time understanding who might want to buy your mushrooms. Visit local markets and stores, chat with people, and learn about their preferences. Think about how you can make your mushrooms stand out, perhaps by focusing on unique types or growing them organically.
- **Space and Tools**: Will you need more space or special tools to grow more mushrooms? Make a list of what you need and check if you need to comply with any local rules or safety standards.
- **Growing Enough Mushrooms**: Consider how many mushrooms you can grow. Remember, it's not just about having enough space, but also time and energy. Think about the scale you're comfortable with.
- **Getting Your Supplies**: Plan out where you'll get your growing supplies like substrates and spawn. You might want to start making your own spawn at home, or connect with trusted suppliers who can provide you with quality materials.

- **Streamlining Your Work**: As you scale up, having a routine can help make your work efficient and consistent. Write down your processes and follow them every time you prepare your substrates, plant your mushrooms, take care of them, and harvest them.

- **Teamwork**: You might need some help as you grow more mushrooms. Consider involving your family or hiring someone who shares your passion for mushroom cultivation. Teach them about your methods and ensure everyone understands the importance of maintaining quality and safety.

- **Finances**: Keep track of what you spend on your mushroom-growing operations and what you earn from selling your mushrooms. This will help you price your mushrooms fairly and keep your hobby-turned-business profitable.

- **Marketing Your Mushrooms**: Think about how to attract people to your mushrooms. You can create a small website, post about your mushrooms on social media, or even join local farmers' markets. Emphasize what makes your mushrooms special!

- **Staying on the Right Side of the Law**: Make sure you're following all the local rules for selling food products. This might involve getting permits, licenses, or certifications.

- **Connecting with Others**: Join a community of mushroom growers. Attend local events, join online groups, and share your experiences and learnings with others. It's a great way to stay up-to-date and get support.

Preparing for Commercial Cultivation

So, you've enjoyed growing mushrooms in your backyard and now you're thinking of growing them on a larger scale? That's fantastic! Let's break down what you need to consider:

1. **Learning More About Your Mushrooms**: Dive deeper into understanding the type of mushrooms you want to grow. Get to know their specific needs and the common problems they might face. You can do this by reading more about them or even joining online workshops and classes.

2. **Space Check**: Check how much space you have for growing your mushrooms. Whether it's a spot in your backyard or an entire room, make sure it's suitable for the kind of mushrooms you want to grow.

3. **Setting Up Your Mushroom "Farm"**: Arrange your space so it provides the right environment for your mushrooms. This could involve setting up shelves for the mushrooms, controlling the temperature and moisture levels, and even adjusting the lighting.

4. **Tools and Supplies**: List down the tools and supplies you need. This could be anything from racks to grow your mushrooms on, to devices that help control temperature and humidity, to the substrates and spawn you'll need to start growing your mushrooms.

5. **Preparing the Substrate**: Decide on the best substrate (the material your mushrooms will grow on) for your mushrooms and how to prepare it. This could involve getting straw,

sawdust, or other organic materials and ensuring they're properly processed and ready for your mushrooms.

6. **Spawn Production**: Think about whether you'll be creating your own mushroom spawn or buying it. If you decide to make your own, you'll need a clean, designated area and some specific equipment.

7. **Environment Watch**: Learn about the specific environmental needs of your mushrooms. This could be monitoring temperature, humidity, or light levels to make sure they're always right for your mushrooms.

8. **Guarding Against Pests and Diseases**: Make a plan to keep your mushrooms healthy and free from pests and diseases. This could involve keeping your growing area clean, checking your mushrooms regularly, and knowing what to do if you spot any problems.

9. **Scheduling and Harvesting**: Create a schedule that includes when to plant your mushrooms, when to expect them to fruit, and when to harvest them. This way, you're always ready for each step.

10. **Keeping Records**: Note down important details about your mushroom growing. This could be when you planted your mushrooms, how they're growing, or how much you harvested. These notes can help you spot patterns or issues that can improve your mushroom farming.

11. **Following the Rules**: Learn about any local rules for selling mushrooms. This could involve food safety standards or labeling requirements.

12. **Making a Business Plan**: Think about your goals and how you'll reach them. This involves deciding where to sell your mushrooms, how much to sell them for, and how to let people know about them.

Remember, growing mushrooms on a larger scale is an exciting new chapter in your mushroom-growing journey. Just like your mushrooms, start small, nurture your process, and watch your business grow!

Making Your Mushroom Business Flourish

1. **Knowing Your Customers**: Understand who's going to buy your mushrooms. This could be local families, restaurants, or grocery stores. Once you know your customers, you can tailor your marketing to them.

2. **Branding**: Come up with a name and a story that makes your mushrooms stand out. It could be something unique about your mushrooms, how you grow them, or even your own journey in starting this business.

3. **Packaging**: Your packaging needs to keep your mushrooms fresh and also catch the eye of potential customers. Don't forget to include all the necessary information on your labels!

4. **Getting the Word Out**: Use different ways to let people know about your mushrooms. You could use social media, local farmers' markets, partnerships with other businesses, or even good old-fashioned advertising. Think about what works best for your customers.

5. **Going Online**: Consider making a website where people can learn more about your mushrooms, how to contact you, and even place orders. Using social media can also help you connect with your customers and share updates.

6. **Connecting with Others**: Get to know others who might help your business grow. This could be chefs, store owners, or other food suppliers. Building these relationships can lead to collaborations and other exciting opportunities.

7. **Educating Customers**: Share with your customers why your mushrooms are special. This could involve sharing tasty recipes, tips for storing and cooking mushrooms, or facts about their health benefits.

8. **Pricing**: Decide on prices that cover your costs, are fair to your customers, and competitive in the market. You could also think about offering different sizes or types of packaging for different needs.

9. **Listening to Customers**: Encourage your customers to give feedback about your mushrooms. This could help you improve your mushrooms or address any issues. Plus, good reviews can help attract new customers!

10. **Building Business Relationships**: Build good relationships with anyone who's part of your mushroom business. This includes suppliers, distributors, or even your local post office. Good relationships can lead to better deals, timely deliveries, and even valuable advice.

11. **Managing Your Finances**: Keep track of what you're spending and earning. This can help you spot ways to save money, set better prices, and understand how your business is doing overall.

12. **Continuous Improvement**: Always look for ways to make your mushrooms and your business better. Keep an eye on what your competitors are doing, what your customers are saying, and what the latest trends are in the food and mushroom world.

Remember, starting a mushroom business is a journey. It'll take time to build up your customer base and find your niche in the market. Just like growing mushrooms, it takes patience, care, and a lot of learning along the way.

Chapter 8

MUSHROOM COOKBOOK

BASICS OF COOKING WITH MUSHROOMS

Cooking with mushrooms can be a delightful and flavorful experience. Whether you're a seasoned chef or a novice in the kitchen, here are some basics to keep in mind when preparing mushrooms:

1. Mushroom Selection

- Look for mushrooms that are firm, plump, and free from bruises or blemishes.
- Different mushroom varieties offer unique flavors and textures. Popular options include button mushrooms, cremini mushrooms, shiitake mushrooms, portobello mushrooms, and oyster mushrooms.

2. Cleaning and Preparing Mushrooms

- Wipe the mushrooms with a damp paper towel or use a soft brush to remove any dirt or debris. Avoid soaking mushrooms in water, as they absorb moisture quickly.
- Depending on the recipe, you may need to trim or remove the tough stems from certain mushroom varieties.

3. Cooking Methods for Mushrooms

- Sautéing: Sautéing mushrooms in a pan with butter or oil over medium-high heat is a popular method. This allows them to release their moisture and develop a golden-brown color and enhanced flavor.
- Roasting: Roasting mushrooms in the oven at a high temperature helps concentrate their flavors and brings out their natural sweetness.
- Grilling: Large, meaty mushrooms like portobello mushrooms are great for grilling. Brush them with marinade or oil and cook them over medium heat until tender and slightly charred.
- Stir-frying: Mushrooms can be stir-fried with other vegetables or proteins to create flavorful dishes. High heat and quick cooking help retain their texture and taste.

4. Flavor Enhancers and Complementary Ingredients

- Garlic and herbs: Garlic, thyme, rosemary, and parsley complement the earthy flavors of mushrooms and add depth to dishes.
- Onions and shallots: Sautéing mushrooms with onions or shallots enhances the overall flavor profile.
- Butter and oil: Butter or cooking oils like olive oil or vegetable oil can be used to cook mushrooms and provide richness.
- Wine or broth: Adding a splash of wine or vegetable broth to the pan while cooking mushrooms can impart additional flavors.

5. Mushroom Recipe Ideas

- Mushroom Risotto: Combine sautéed mushrooms with creamy Arborio rice, broth, and Parmesan cheese for a delicious and comforting dish.
- Mushroom Pasta: Toss cooked pasta with sautéed mushrooms, garlic, herbs, and a drizzle of olive oil for a simple yet flavorful meal.
- Stuffed Mushrooms: Remove the stems from large mushroom caps, stuff them with a filling of your choice (such as cheese, breadcrumbs, and herbs), and bake until golden and bubbling.
- Mushroom Soup: Sauté mushrooms with onions and garlic, then simmer them in vegetable or chicken broth. Puree for a creamy mushroom soup.

- Mushroom Stir-Fry: Combine mushrooms with an assortment of vegetables, soy sauce, and spices for a quick and nutritious stir-fry.

Preparing Mushrooms for Cooking

Preparing mushrooms for cooking involves a few essential steps to ensure they are clean and ready to be incorporated into your recipes. Here's a guide on how to prepare mushrooms:

1. Selecting Mushrooms

- Choose fresh mushrooms: Look for mushrooms that are firm, plump, and free from any signs of decay or discoloration. Avoid mushrooms with slimy or dried-out surfaces.

2. Cleaning Mushrooms

- Gently clean the mushrooms: Using a soft brush or a damp paper towel, carefully remove any dirt or debris from the mushroom caps and stems. Avoid rinsing them with water, as mushrooms are porous and can easily absorb moisture, which may affect their texture and flavor.

3. Trimming and Cutting

- Trim the stems: Depending on the recipe and the type of mushrooms you're using, you may need to trim the tough or woody ends of the stems. For delicate mushrooms like button mushrooms or cremini mushrooms, you can leave the stems intact.
- Slice or dice as desired: Once the mushrooms are cleaned and trimmed, you can slice them, dice them, or leave them whole, depending on your recipe and personal preference.

4. Precooking Methods (optional)

- Some recipes may call for precooking the mushrooms to enhance their flavor or texture. Here are a couple of common methods:
- Sautéing: Heat a bit of oil or butter in a pan over medium heat. Add the sliced or diced mushrooms and cook them until they release their moisture and turn golden brown. This can help intensify their flavor and remove excess moisture.
- Blanching: Bring a pot of water to a boil and briefly submerge the mushrooms for about 1 minute. Then, transfer them to an ice bath to stop the cooking process. Blanching can help soften the mushrooms slightly and prepare them for further cooking.

5. Ready for Cooking

- Once your mushrooms are cleaned, trimmed, and prepped (if necessary), they are ready to be used in your recipes. Add them to sauces, soups, stir-fries, pasta dishes, or any other recipe that calls for mushrooms.

Pairing Mushrooms with Other Ingredients

1. Garlic and Onions

Mushrooms and garlic are a classic combination. The earthiness of mushrooms is beautifully complemented by the pungent and aromatic flavors of garlic. Sautéing mushrooms with minced garlic and onions creates a flavorful base for many dishes.

2. Fresh Herbs

Herbs like thyme, rosemary, sage, and parsley add freshness and complexity to mushroom dishes. Sprinkle chopped herbs over sautéed mushrooms or incorporate them into sauces, stuffings, or risottos for an added layer of flavor.

3. Butter and Olive Oil

Mushrooms have a natural affinity for butter and olive oil. These fats help bring out the richness and intensify the flavors of mushrooms. Sautéing mushrooms in butter or drizzling them with extra-virgin olive oil adds depth to the dish.

4. Cream and Cheese

Creamy textures and cheesy flavors complement the mushrooms well. Adding a splash of cream to mushroom sauces or incorporating cheeses like Parmesan, Gruyère, or goat cheese can elevate the dish's creaminess and richness.

5. Wine and Broth

Mushrooms have a unique ability to absorb flavors, making them perfect for cooking in wine or broth. Red wine, white wine, or mushroom broth can enhance the savory notes of mushrooms and create a delicious base for sauces, soups, or stews.

6. Leafy Greens

Combining mushrooms with leafy greens such as spinach, kale, or Swiss chard adds color, texture, and nutritional value to your dishes. Sautéed mushrooms and greens work well together in stir-fries, pasta dishes, or as a filling for omelets.

7. Grains

Mushrooms can be paired with various grains like rice, quinoa, barley, or pasta. They add a savory element and create a hearty, satisfying meal. Mushrooms can be incorporated into risottos, grain bowls, or stuffed mushroom caps with grain fillings.

8. Citrus

Brightening the earthy flavors of mushrooms with a splash of citrus juice or zest can add a refreshing and tangy note to your dishes. Lemon, lime, or orange can balance the richness and bring a vibrant touch to mushroom salads, sauces, or marinades.

9. Nuts

Adding toasted nuts, such as almonds, walnuts, or pine nuts, to mushroom dishes brings a delightful crunch and nutty flavor. They can be sprinkled over salads, mixed into stuffings, or incorporated into grain-based dishes.

10. Umami Ingredients

Mushrooms naturally possess umami, the savory taste that adds depth to dishes. Enhance this umami flavor by pairing mushrooms with ingredients like soy sauce, miso paste, balsamic vinegar, or Worcestershire sauce. These ingredients amplify the savory profile of mushrooms and create a robust taste.

MUSHROOM RECIPES

Appetizers and Side Dishes

Stuffed Mushrooms

Prep Time: 15 minutes

Cook Time: 20 minutes

Serving Size: 4-6 servings

Ingredients:

- 20 large white button mushrooms
- 1/2 cup breadcrumbs
- 1/4 cup grated Parmesan cheese
- 2 cloves garlic, minced
- 2 tablespoons chopped fresh parsley
- 2 tablespoons olive oil
- Salt and pepper to taste

Instructions:

1. Preheat the oven to 375°F (190°C) and line a baking sheet with parchment paper.
2. Clean the mushrooms and remove the stems. Set the caps aside.
3. Finely chop the mushroom stems and place them in a bowl.
4. Add breadcrumbs, Parmesan cheese, minced garlic, chopped parsley, olive oil, salt, and pepper to the bowl. Mix well to combine.
5. Stuff each mushroom cap with the breadcrumb mixture and place them on the prepared baking sheet.
6. Bake for about 20 minutes or until the mushrooms are tender and the tops are golden brown.
7. Serve the stuffed mushrooms as a delicious appetizer or side dish.

Nutritional facts:

- Calories: 120
- Fat: 6g
- Carbohydrates: 12g
- Protein: 6g

Mushroom Bruschetta

Prep Time: 10 minutes

Cook Time: 15 minutes

Serving Size: 4 servings

Ingredients:

- 4 slices of baguette or crusty bread
- 1 cup sliced mushrooms (such as cremini or shiitake)
- 2 tablespoons olive oil
- 1 clove garlic, minced
- 1 tablespoon balsamic vinegar
- 2 tablespoons chopped fresh basil
- Salt and pepper to taste

Instructions:

1. Preheat the oven to 400°F (200°C).
2. Brush the bread slices with olive oil and place them on a baking sheet. Toast in the oven for about 5 minutes until lightly golden.
3. In a skillet, heat olive oil over medium heat. Add the sliced mushrooms and cook for about 5-7 minutes until they are tender and lightly browned.
4. Add minced garlic to the skillet and sauté for an additional 1 minute.
5. Stir in balsamic vinegar, chopped basil, salt, and pepper. Cook for another 2 minutes, allowing the flavors to meld together.
6. Remove the bread slices from the oven and top them with the sautéed mushroom mixture.
7. Serve the mushroom bruschetta as a flavorful appetizer or side dish.

Nutritional facts:

- Calories: 150
- Fat: 8g
- Carbohydrates: 15g
- Protein: 4g

Creamy Mushroom Dip

Prep Time: 10 minutes

Cook Time: 20 minutes

Serving Size: 6 servings

Ingredients:

- 2 cups sliced mushrooms (such as button or cremini)
- 1 small onion, finely chopped
- 2 cloves garlic, minced
- 2 tablespoons butter
- 4 ounces of cream cheese
- 1/4 cup sour cream
- 1/4 cup grated Parmesan cheese
- 1 tablespoon chopped fresh parsley
- Salt and pepper to taste

Instructions:

1. In a skillet, melt the butter over medium heat. Add the chopped onion and minced garlic. Sauté until the onion is translucent and fragrant.
2. Add the sliced mushrooms to the skillet and cook until they are tender and lightly browned.
3. Reduce the heat to low and add cream cheese, sour cream, grated Parmesan cheese, chopped parsley, salt, and pepper to the skillet. Stir well until the cheeses are melted, and the ingredients are combined.
4. Continue to cook for an additional 5 minutes, allowing the flavors to meld together.
5. Transfer the creamy mushroom dip to a serving bowl and garnish with additional parsley, if desired.
6. Serve the dip with crackers, bread, or vegetable sticks as a delightful appetizer.

Nutritional facts:

- Calories: 160
- Fat: 13g
- Carbohydrates: 6g
- Protein: 5g

Main Dishes

Mushroom Risotto

Prep Time: 10 minutes
Cook Time: 30 minutes
Serving Size: 4 servings

Ingredients:

- 1 cup Arborio rice
- 4 cups vegetable or mushroom broth
- 1 cup sliced mushrooms (such as shiitake or cremini)
- 1 small onion, finely chopped
- 2 cloves garlic, minced
- 1/4 cup grated Parmesan cheese
- 2 tablespoons butter
- 2 tablespoons olive oil
- 1/4 cup dry white wine (optional)
- Salt and pepper to taste
- Chopped fresh parsley for garnish

Instructions:

1. In a large saucepan, heat olive oil and butter over medium heat. Add the chopped onion and minced garlic. Sauté until the onion is translucent and fragrant.

2. Add the sliced mushrooms to the saucepan and cook until they are tender and lightly browned.

3. Add Arborio rice to the saucepan and stir to coat the rice with the mushroom mixture.

4. If using wine, pour it into the saucepan and cook until the liquid is absorbed.

5. Gradually add vegetable or mushroom broth, about 1/2 cup at a time, stirring constantly until the liquid is absorbed before adding more. Continue this process until the rice is cooked al dente and has a creamy consistency.

6. Stir in grated Parmesan cheese and season with salt and pepper.

7. Remove from heat and let the risotto rest for a few minutes.

8. Serve the mushroom risotto garnished with chopped fresh parsley.

Nutritional facts:

- Calories: 300
- Fat: 10g
- Carbohydrates: 45g
- Protein: 8g

Mushroom and Spinach Stuffed Chicken Breast

Prep Time: 15 minutes
Cook Time: 30 minutes
Serving Size: 4 servings

- Ingredients:
- 4 boneless, skinless chicken breasts
- 1 cup sliced mushrooms (such as cremini or button)
- 2 cups fresh spinach leaves
- 1/2 cup shredded mozzarella cheese
- 2 cloves garlic, minced
- 2 tablespoons olive oil
- Salt and pepper to taste

Instructions:

1. Preheat the oven to 375°F (190°C).
2. In a skillet, heat olive oil over medium heat. Add the sliced mushrooms and minced garlic. Cook until the mushrooms are tender and lightly browned.
3. Add the fresh spinach leaves to the skillet and cook until wilted.
4. Season the chicken breasts with salt and pepper. Cut a slit in the side of each chicken breast to create a pocket for the filling.
5. Stuff each chicken breast with the mushroom and spinach mixture, then top with shredded mozzarella cheese.
6. Secure the chicken breasts with toothpicks to hold the filling in place.
7. Heat olive oil in an oven-safe skillet over medium-high heat. Sear the chicken breasts on each side until golden brown.
8. Transfer the skillet to the preheated oven and bake for about 20 minutes or until the chicken is cooked through and the cheese is melted and bubbly.
9. Remove the toothpicks before serving.

Nutritional facts:

- Calories: 320
- Fat: 14g
- Carbohydrates: 4g
- Protein: 42g

Mushroom and Gruyère Quiche

Prep Time: 15 minutes
Cook Time: 45 minutes
Serving Size: 6 servings

Ingredients:

- 1 pre-made pie crust
- 1 cup sliced mushrooms (such as cremini or shiitake)
- 1 small onion, finely chopped
- 2 cloves garlic, minced
- 1 cup shredded Gruyère cheese
- 4 large eggs
- 1 cup heavy cream
- Salt and pepper to taste
- Chopped fresh parsley for garnish

Instructions:

1. Preheat the oven to 375°F (190°C).
2. Roll out the pre-made pie crust and place it in a pie dish. Trim any excess crust hanging over the edges.
3. In a skillet, heat olive oil over medium heat. Add the chopped onion and minced garlic. Sauté until the onion is translucent and fragrant.
4. Add the sliced mushrooms to the skillet and cook until they are tender and lightly browned.
5. Spread the sautéed mushroom mixture evenly over the pie crust. Sprinkle shredded Gruyère cheese on top.
6. In a separate bowl, whisk together eggs, heavy cream, salt, and pepper. Pour the mixture over the mushrooms and cheese into the pie crust.
7. Place the quiche in the preheated oven and bake for about 40-45 minutes or until the center is set and the top is golden brown.
8. Remove from the oven and let it cool slightly before slicing.
9. Garnish with chopped fresh parsley before serving.

Nutritional facts:

- Calories: 380
- Fat: 28g
- Carbohydrates: 17g
- Protein: 15g

Soups and Stews

Creamy Mushroom Soup

Prep Time: 15 minutes

Cook Time: 30 minutes

Serving Size: 4 servings

Ingredients:

- 1 pound sliced mushrooms (such as cremini or button)
- 1 small onion, finely chopped
- 2 cloves garlic, minced
- 4 cups vegetable or mushroom broth
- 1 cup heavy cream
- 2 tablespoons butter
- 2 tablespoons all-purpose flour
- 1 tablespoon chopped fresh thyme
- Salt and pepper to taste

Instructions:

1. In a large pot, melt the butter over medium heat. Add the chopped onion and minced garlic. Sauté until the onion is translucent and fragrant.
2. Add the sliced mushrooms to the pot and cook until they are tender and lightly browned.
3. Sprinkle the flour over the mushrooms and stir well to coat.
4. Gradually pour in the vegetable or mushroom broth, stirring continuously to prevent lumps from forming.
5. Bring the mixture to a simmer and cook for about 15 minutes, allowing the flavors to meld together.
6. Stir in the heavy cream and chopped fresh thyme. Season with salt and pepper.
7. Continue to cook for an additional 5 minutes, stirring occasionally.
8. Remove from heat and let the soup cool slightly.
9. Use an immersion blender or transfer the soup to a blender to puree until smooth and creamy.
10. Return the soup to the pot and heat gently before serving.

Nutritional facts:

- Calories: 280
- Fat: 22g
- Carbohydrates: 16g
- Protein: 6g

Wild Mushroom and Barley Stew

Prep Time: 15 minutes
Cook Time: 1 hour
Serving Size: 6 servings

Ingredients:

- 1 cup mixed wild mushrooms (such as shiitake, oyster, and porcini), sliced
- 1 cup sliced cremini mushrooms
- 1 onion, finely chopped
- 2 cloves garlic, minced
- 1 carrot, diced
- 1 celery stalk, diced
- 1 cup pearl barley
- 4 cups vegetable or mushroom broth
- 1 tablespoon chopped fresh thyme
- 1 tablespoon chopped fresh rosemary
- Salt and pepper to taste
- Chopped fresh parsley for garnish

Instructions:

1. In a large pot, heat olive oil over medium heat. Add the chopped onion and minced garlic. Sauté until the onion is translucent and fragrant.

2. Add the sliced wild mushrooms, cremini mushrooms, carrots, and celery to the pot. Cook until the vegetables are slightly softened.
3. Stir in the pearl barley, vegetable, or mushroom broth, chopped fresh thyme, and chopped fresh rosemary.
4. Bring the mixture to a boil, then reduce the heat to low. Cover the pot and simmer for about 45 minutes to 1 hour, or until the barley is tender and the flavors have melded together.
5. Season the stew with salt and pepper to taste.
6. Serve the wild mushroom and barley stew garnished with chopped fresh parsley.

Nutritional facts:

- Calories: 290
- Fat: 2g
- Carbohydrates: 60g
- Protein: 9g

Mushroom and Lentil Soup

Prep Time: 15 minutes
Cook Time: 45 minutes
Serving Size: 6 servings

Ingredients:

- 1 cup green lentils, rinsed
- 1 cup sliced mushrooms (such as cremini or shiitake)
- 1 onion, finely chopped
- 2 cloves garlic, minced
- 2 carrots, diced
- 2 celery stalks, diced
- 4 cups vegetable or mushroom broth
- 1 tablespoon tomato paste
- 1 teaspoon dried thyme
- 1 teaspoon smoked paprika
- Salt and pepper to taste

- Chopped fresh parsley for garnish

Instructions:

1. In a large pot, heat olive oil over medium heat. Add the chopped onion and minced garlic. Sauté until the onion is translucent and fragrant.

2. Add the sliced mushrooms, diced carrots, and diced celery to the pot. Cook until the vegetables are slightly softened.
3. Stir in the green lentils, vegetable or mushroom broth, tomato paste, dried thyme, and smoked paprika.
4. Bring the mixture to a boil, then reduce the heat to low. Cover the pot and simmer for about 30-40 minutes or until the lentils are tender.
5. Season the soup with salt and pepper to taste.
6. Serve the mushroom and lentil soup garnished with chopped fresh parsley.

Nutritional facts:

- Calories: 220
- Fat: 1g
- Carbohydrates: 43g
- Protein: 12g

MEDICINAL MUSHROOM RECIPES

Medicinal mushrooms have been used for centuries in various traditional medicine practices for their potential health benefits. These mushrooms contain bioactive compounds that may support immune function, reduce inflammation, and promote overall well-being. Some popular medicinal mushrooms include Reishi, Chaga, Lion's Mane, Cordyceps, and Turkey Tail. Incorporating these mushrooms into your diet can be done through extracts, teas, and various recipes.

Preparing Medicinal Mushroom Extracts and Teas

To harness the potential health benefits of medicinal mushrooms, extracts, and teas can be prepared. These preparations involve extracting the bioactive compounds from the mushrooms to create a concentrated form that can be easily consumed. Here is a more detailed explanation of how to prepare medicinal mushroom extracts and teas:

Medicinal Mushroom Extracts:

1. Choose the Medicinal Mushrooms: Start by selecting the medicinal mushrooms you want to use for your extract. Popular choices include Reishi, Chaga, Lion's Mane, Cordyceps, and Turkey Tail. Ensure that the mushrooms are of high quality, preferably sourced from reputable suppliers.

2. Preparation of Mushrooms: If using dried mushrooms, grind them into a fine powder using a coffee grinder or blender. If using fresh mushrooms, finely chop them. The surface area of the mushrooms affects the extraction process, so the finer the powder or, the smaller the pieces, the more efficient the extraction will be.

3. Water Extraction Method: In a pot, add water and bring it to a boil. Add the powdered or chopped mushrooms to the boiling water and reduce the heat to low. Simmer the mixture for about 1-2 hours, allowing the water to extract the beneficial compounds from the mushrooms. The longer the simmering time, the more concentrated the extract will be. Stir occasionally to ensure proper extraction.

4. Straining and Storing: After simmering, strain the liquid through a fine-mesh sieve or cheesecloth to remove any solid particles. Press the mushrooms against the sieve or cheesecloth to extract as much liquid as possible. Transfer the liquid extract to a clean container, preferably a glass jar. Store the extract in the refrigerator for up to a week, or freeze it in ice cube trays for longer-term storage.

5. Usage: Medicinal mushroom extracts can be consumed directly or incorporated into recipes such as smoothies, teas, or soups. Follow the recommended dosage guidelines for the specific mushroom you are using. It is advisable to start with a small dosage and gradually increase it as needed.

Medicinal Mushroom Teas:

1. Choose the Mushrooms: Similar to making extracts, choose the medicinal mushrooms you want to use. Dried mushrooms are commonly used for making teas, but fresh mushrooms can also be used.

2. Preparation of Mushrooms: If using dried mushrooms, break them into smaller pieces to increase the surface area for extraction. If using fresh mushrooms, thinly slice them.

3. Water-to-Mushroom Ratio: The water-to-mushroom ratio may vary depending on the mushroom variety and personal preference. As a general guideline, use 1-2 tablespoons of dried mushrooms or 1/2 to 1 cup of fresh mushrooms per 4 cups of water. Adjust the ratio to achieve the desired strength and flavor.

4. Steeping Process: In a pot, add water and bring it to a boil. Once the water reaches a boil, reduce the heat to low and add the mushrooms. Simmer the mushrooms for about 20-30 minutes, or until the water has reduced and the flavors have infused. Longer steeping times will result in stronger tea.

5. Straining and Serving: After steeping, strain the tea through a fine-mesh sieve or cheesecloth to remove any mushroom particles. Sweeteners such as honey or stevia can be added to enhance the taste if desired. Serve the tea hot or chilled, depending on personal preference.

6. Usage: Medicinal mushroom teas can be enjoyed on their own or combined with other herbal teas to create flavorful blends. They can be consumed daily or as needed to support health and well-being. Follow the recommended dosage guidelines for the specific mushroom you are using.

Below are two medicinal mushroom extract recipes and two medicinal mushroom tea recipes for you to try:

Reishi Mushroom Extract

Prep Time: 10 minutes

Cook Time: 2 hours

Serving Size: Varies

Ingredients:

- 1 cup dried Reishi mushroom slices
- 4 cups water

Instructions:

1. In a pot, bring 4 cups of water to a boil.
2. Add the dried Reishi mushroom slices to the boiling water and reduce the heat to low.
3. Simmer the mixture for approximately 2 hours, allowing the water to extract the beneficial compounds from the mushrooms.
4. Stir occasionally to ensure proper extraction.
5. After simmering, remove the pot from heat and let the mixture cool.
6. Strain the liquid through a fine-mesh sieve or cheesecloth into a clean glass jar.
7. Store the Reishi mushroom extract in the refrigerator for up to a week.
8. Consume as desired, starting with a small dosage and gradually increasing if needed.

Chaga Mushroom Extract

Prep Time: 10 minutes

Cook Time: 4-6 hours

Serving Size: Varies

Ingredients:

- 1 cup dried Chaga mushroom chunks
- 4 cups water

Instructions:

1. Place the dried Chaga mushroom chunks in a coffee grinder or blender and pulse until they form a fine powder.
2. In a pot, bring 4 cups of water to a boil.
3. Add the powdered Chaga mushroom to the boiling water and reduce the heat to low.
4. Simmer the mixture for 4-6 hours, allowing the water to extract the beneficial compounds from the mushrooms.
5. Stir occasionally to ensure proper extraction.
6. After simmering, remove the pot from heat and let the mixture cool.
7. Strain the liquid through a fine-mesh sieve or cheesecloth into a clean glass jar.
8. Store the Chaga mushroom extract in the refrigerator for up to a week.
9. Consume as desired, starting with a small dosage and gradually increasing if needed.

Lion's Mane Mushroom Tea

Prep Time: 5 minutes

Cook Time: 15 minutes

Serving Size: 2 servings

Ingredients:

- 2 cups water
- 2 teaspoons dried Lion's Mane mushroom powder
- Optional: honey or sweetener of choice

Instructions:

1. In a pot, bring 2 cups of water to a boil.
2. Add the dried Lion's Mane mushroom powder to the boiling water.
3. Reduce the heat to low and simmer for approximately 15 minutes.
4. Remove the pot from heat and let the tea steep for a few minutes.
5. Strain the tea through a fine-mesh sieve or tea strainer into cups.
6. Add honey or sweetener if desired, and stir well.
7. Serve the Lion's Mane mushroom tea hot, and enjoy.

Cordyceps Mushroom Tea

Prep Time: 5 minutes

Cook Time: 15 minutes

Serving Size: 2 servings

Ingredients:

- 2 cups water
- 2 teaspoons dried Cordyceps mushroom powder
- Optional: lemon slices or sweetener of choice

Instructions:

1. In a pot, bring 2 cups of water to a boil.
2. Add the dried Cordyceps mushroom powder to the boiling water.
3. Reduce the heat to low and simmer for approximately 15 minutes.
4. Remove the pot from heat and let the tea steep for a few minutes.
5. Strain the tea through a fine-mesh sieve or tea strainer into cups.
6. Add lemon slices or sweetener if desired, and stir well.
7. Serve the Cordyceps mushroom tea hot, and enjoy.

Remember to adjust the dosages and flavors according to your preferences and consult with a healthcare professional or herbalist for personalized advice and dosages, especially if you have any underlying health conditions or are taking medications.

Recipes Incorporating Medicinal Mushrooms

Recipes Incorporating Medicinal Mushrooms

Incorporating medicinal mushrooms into recipes allows for both their potential health benefits and delicious flavors to be enjoyed. Here are a few recipe ideas that incorporate medicinal mushrooms:

Mushroom and Spinach Stuffed Portobello Mushrooms

Prep Time: 15 minutes

Cook Time: 20 minutes

Serving Size: 2 servings

Ingredients:

- 2 large Portobello mushrooms
- 1 cup sliced mushrooms (e.g., Reishi, Chaga, or Lion's Mane)
- 1 cup fresh spinach leaves
- 2 cloves garlic, minced
- 2 tablespoons olive oil
- Salt and pepper to taste

Instructions:

1. Preheat the oven to 375°F (190°C).
2. Clean the Portobello mushrooms and remove the stems. Place them on a baking sheet.
3. In a skillet, heat olive oil over medium heat. Add the sliced mushrooms and minced garlic. Cook until the mushrooms are tender and lightly browned.
4. Add the fresh spinach leaves to the skillet and cook until wilted.
5. Season with salt and pepper to taste.
6. Spoon the mushroom and spinach mixture into the Portobello mushroom caps.
7. Place the stuffed Portobello mushrooms on the baking sheet and bake for about 20 minutes or until the mushrooms are tender.
8. Serve as a flavorful and nutritious main dish.

Nutritional facts:

- Calories: 180
- Fat: 12g
- Carbohydrates: 12g
- Protein: 10g

Reishi Hot Chocolate

Prep Time: 5 minutes

Cook Time: 5 minutes

Serving Size: 1 serving

Ingredients:

- 1 cup milk (dairy or plant-based)
- 1 tablespoon cocoa powder
- 1 tablespoon maple syrup or sweetener of choice
- 1/2 teaspoon Reishi mushroom extract powder
- Optional: whipped cream or marshmallows for topping

Instructions:

1. In a small saucepan, heat the milk over medium-low heat until hot but not boiling.
2. Whisk in the cocoa powder, maple syrup, and Reishi mushroom extract powder until well combined.
3. Continue to heat and whisk until the mixture is hot and frothy.
4. Pour the Reishi hot chocolate into a mug and top with whipped cream or marshmallows if desired.
5. Serve and enjoy the comforting and health-supportive beverage.

Nutritional facts:

- Calories: 150
- Fat: 5g
- Carbohydrates: 22g
- Protein: 8g

Cordyceps Energy Balls

Prep Time: 15 minutes

Cook Time: No cooking required

Serving Size: Approximately 12 energy balls

Ingredients:

- 1 cup dates, pitted
- 1/2 cup nuts of your choice (e.g., almonds, cashews)
- 1/4 cup shredded coconut
- 2 tablespoons cacao powder
- 1 tablespoon Cordyceps mushroom extract powder
- Optional: additional shredded coconut for coating

Instructions:

1. In a food processor, combine the dates, nuts, shredded coconut, cacao powder, and Cordyceps mushroom extract powder.
2. Process until the mixture comes together and forms a sticky dough.
3. Roll the dough into small balls about 1 inch in diameter.
4. Optional: Roll the energy balls in additional shredded coconut to coat the exterior.
5. Place the energy balls in an airtight container and refrigerate for at least 1 hour to firm up.
6. Enjoy these nutritious and energizing Cordyceps-infused snacks on the go.

Nutritional facts (per energy ball):

- Calories: 100
- Fat: 5g
- Carbohydrates: 15g
- Protein: 2g

These recipes showcase the versatility of incorporating medicinal mushrooms into your daily meals. By following these recipes, you can explore the potential health benefits of medicinal mushrooms while indulging in delicious and nourishing dishes. Remember to source high-quality mushrooms and adjust the recipes according to your personal preferences and dietary needs.

Chapter 9

MUSHROOM ENCYCLOPEDIA

COMPREHENSIVE LIST OF MUSHROOM SPECIES

Edible Mushroom Species

There is a wide variety of edible mushroom species available for consumption, each with its own unique flavors, textures, and culinary uses. Here is a list of some popular edible mushroom species:

1. Agaricus bisporus (Button Mushroom)

The common white button mushroom, crimini (brown) mushroom, and portobello mushroom are all variations of Agaricus bisporus. They have a mild flavor and can be used in various dishes.

2. Pleurotus ostreatus (Oyster Mushroom)

Oyster mushrooms are known for their delicate flavor and velvety texture. They come in different colors and are used in stir-fries, soups, and other dishes.

3. Lentinula edodes (Shiitake Mushroom)

Shiitake mushrooms have a distinct umami flavor and a meaty texture. They are widely used in Asian cuisine and are often dried for extended shelf life.

4. Hericium erinaceus (Lion's Mane Mushroom)

Lion's Mane mushrooms have a unique appearance with cascading spines. They have a mild, seafood-like flavor and a delicate texture. They can be cooked or used raw in salads.

5. Cantharellus cibarius (Chanterelle Mushroom)

Chanterelles are highly prized for their fruity, apricot-like flavor and meaty texture. They are often used in gourmet dishes and pair well with cream-based sauces.

Medicinal Mushroom Species

1. Ganoderma lucidum (Reishi Mushroom)

Reishi mushrooms are highly regarded for their potential immune-enhancing properties. They are also believed to have anti-inflammatory, antioxidant, and stress-reducing effects.

2. Cordyceps sinensis (Caterpillar Fungus)

Cordyceps are known for their adaptogenic properties, which can help improve energy, endurance, and athletic performance. They are also believed to support respiratory health and immune function.

3. Trametes versicolor (Turkey Tail Mushroom)

Turkey tail mushrooms are rich in polysaccharides and are known for their potential immunomodulatory effects. They are often used as adjunctive therapy for cancer and to support immune function.

4. Inonotus obliquus (Chaga Mushroom)

Chaga mushrooms are rich in antioxidants and have been studied for their potential anticancer, anti-inflammatory, and immune-enhancing effects. They are also used to support skin health.

5. Grifola frondosa (Maitake Mushroom)

Maitake mushrooms are rich in beta-glucans and have been studied for their potential antitumor and immunomodulatory effects. They are also used to support overall immune health.

DETAILED DESCRIPTIONS AND ILLUSTRATIONS

Physical Characteristics

1. Agaricus bisporus (Button Mushroom)

- The button mushroom has a smooth, rounded cap with a creamy-white or light brown color.
- The cap can range in size from small buttons to larger, fully expanded mushrooms.
- Its gills start off pink and then turn dark brown as the mushroom matures.
- The stem is firm and white, with a slightly enlarged base.

2. Pleurotus ostreatus (Oyster Mushroom)

- Oyster mushrooms have a unique appearance with a fan-shaped cap and a delicate, oyster-like texture.
- The cap can vary in color, ranging from white to gray, brown, or even blue-gray, depending on the species and growing conditions.
- They have decurrent gills, which means the gills are attached to and run down the stem.
- The stem is often absent or very short, and when present, it is usually off-center and tough.

3. Lentinula edodes (Shiitake Mushroom)

- Shiitake mushrooms have a distinct umbrella-shaped cap with a brown color.
- The cap surface is often dry and has a slightly wrinkled appearance.
- The gills underneath the cap are cream-colored when young and turn dark brown as the mushroom matures.
- The stem is thick, firm, and brown, with a white ring around the top.

4. Hericium erinaceus (Lion's Mane Mushroom)

- Lion's Mane mushrooms have a unique appearance with cascading, elongated spines that resemble a lion's mane or a pom-pom.
- The spines are usually white or cream-colored.
- They can vary in size, ranging from small, compact clusters to larger, more spread-out formations.
- Lion's Mane mushrooms have no gills or caps.

5. Cantharellus cibarius (Chanterelle Mushroom)

- Chanterelle mushrooms have a distinctive funnel or trumpet shape with a smooth cap and a wavy margin.
- The cap can range in color from vibrant yellow to orange or reddish-orange.

- They have a fleshy texture, and their undersides feature ridges instead of traditional gills.

6. Ganoderma lucidum (Reishi Mushroom)

- The cap of Reishi mushrooms is usually fan-shaped or kidney-shaped and can range in color from reddish-brown to dark brown. The surface is smooth and shiny.
- The spores of Reishi mushrooms are brown.
- Reishi mushrooms have a short, stubby stem that is typically off-center or eccentric.

7. Cordyceps sinensis (Caterpillar Fungus)

- The fruiting body of Cordyceps sinensis consists of elongated, cylindrical structures that are dark brown to black in color. They have a sinuous or curved shape and can reach several centimeters in length.

8. Trametes versicolor (Turkey Tail Mushroom)

- The cap of Turkey Tail mushrooms is fan-shaped and has multiple concentric bands of various colors. The colors can include shades of brown, tan, white, and blueish-gray.
- The spores of Turkey Tail mushrooms are white.
- The surface of the cap is often velvety or finely fuzzy.

9. Inonotus obliquus (Chaga Mushroom)

- Chaga mushrooms have a unique appearance, often resembling a black, burnt, or charred mass on the bark of birch trees.
- The exterior of the mushroom is hard and crusty, with a dark black color.
- The interior of the mushroom is typically orange-brown and has a cork-like texture.
- Chaga mushrooms can vary in size, ranging from small chunks to larger formations.

10. Grifola frondosa (Maitake Mushroom)

- Maitake mushrooms have multiple overlapping layers of fan-shaped caps. The caps are brownish in color and have a wavy or crinkled surface.
- The caps are fleshy and firm, with a somewhat fibrous texture.

Habitat and Growth Conditions

1. Agaricus bisporus (Button Mushroom)

- Button mushrooms are cultivated worldwide and can also be found growing in the wild.
- They typically grow in nutrient-rich soil and are commonly associated with grassy areas or woodlands.
- The mushrooms prefer a cool, moist environment and thrive in temperatures between 55 and 65°F (13 and 18°C).
- They are often grown indoors in controlled environments, such as mushroom farms.

2. Pleurotus ostreatus (Oyster Mushroom)

- Oyster mushrooms are found worldwide and can grow in various habitats, including woodlands, forests, and decaying wood.
- They are also commonly cultivated on a commercial scale.
- Oyster mushrooms thrive in moderate temperatures and prefer high humidity levels.
- They are often grown on substrates like straw, sawdust, or wood chips.

3. Lentinula edodes (Shiitake Mushroom)

- Shiitake mushrooms are native to East Asia but are now cultivated globally.
- They are typically grown on logs or sawdust blocks made from hardwood trees like oak, beech, or maple.
- Shiitake cultivation requires specific temperature and humidity conditions, often mimicking the natural growth environment.
- They can also be found growing in the wild on dead or decaying wood.

4. Hericium erinaceus (Lion's Mane Mushroom)

- Lion's Mane mushrooms are found in both temperate and tropical regions, growing on hardwood trees, especially beech, oak, and maple.
- They are also cultivated on sawdust, logs, or specialized substrates in controlled environments.
- The mushrooms require high humidity and cooler temperatures for optimal growth.

5. Cantharellus cibarius (Chanterelle Mushroom)

- Chanterelle mushrooms are found in forests and woodlands, often growing in close association with trees like oaks, pines, or birches.
- They prefer well-drained soil and are commonly found in mossy areas.
- Chanterelles have a mycorrhizal relationship with trees, forming mutually beneficial associations.

6. Ganoderma lucidum (Reishi Mushroom)

- Reishi mushrooms are often found growing on decaying hardwood trees, particularly oak, and maple. They have a preference for wooded areas and are commonly found in forests.
- Reishi mushrooms thrive in temperate and subtropical climates. They require a moist environment and tend to grow during the warmer months.

7. Cordyceps sinensis (Caterpillar Fungus)

- Cordyceps sinensis is a parasitic fungus that grows on the larvae of insects, especially caterpillars. They are commonly found in mountainous regions and alpine meadows.
- Cordyceps sinensis requires specific environmental conditions, including cool temperatures, high altitude, and a symbiotic relationship with its host insect. It is predominantly found in regions like the Himalayas and Tibetan Plateau.

8. Trametes versicolor (Turkey Tail Mushroom)

- Turkey Tail mushrooms are widespread and can be found in various habitats. They commonly grow on dead hardwood trees, fallen logs, and decaying wood in forests.
- Turkey Tail mushrooms are adaptable and can grow in both temperate and tropical climates. They are often found throughout the year, but their growth is more prevalent during the wetter seasons.

9. Inonotus obliquus (Chaga Mushroom)

- Chaga mushrooms are predominantly found in regions with cold climates, such as Siberia, Canada, Alaska, and parts of Northern Europe.
- They primarily grow on birch trees, specifically on wounded or stressed areas of the tree bark.
- Chaga mushrooms form a symbiotic relationship with the host tree, drawing nutrients from it while also potentially benefiting the tree by promoting healing.

10. Grifola frondosa (Maitake Mushroom)

- Maitake mushrooms are typically found growing at the base of oak, elm, and beech trees. They are commonly found in deciduous forests.
- Maitake mushrooms prefer a temperate climate with cool temperatures. They require a cool and moist environment for growth.

Potential Uses and Warnings

Here are the potential uses and some warnings associated with the medicinal mushroom species mentioned earlier:

1. Agaricus bisporus (Button Mushroom)

- Button mushrooms are one of the most widely consumed mushrooms and are versatile in cooking.
- They have a mild flavor that pairs well with various dishes, including soups, stir-fries, salads, and sauces.
- Button mushrooms are low in calories and a good source of nutrients such as B vitamins, selenium, and potassium.
- While generally safe for consumption, some individuals may experience digestive issues or allergic reactions to mushrooms. It's important to cook them thoroughly before eating.

2. Pleurotus ostreatus (Oyster Mushroom)

- Oyster mushrooms have a delicate, mild flavor and a tender texture, making them suitable for various culinary applications.
- They are commonly used in stir-fries, soups, and pasta dishes and as a meat substitute in vegetarian and vegan recipes.
- Oyster mushrooms are a good source of protein, fiber, and several vitamins and minerals.
- While generally safe to consume, it's important to properly identify wild mushrooms and avoid consumption if unsure, as some toxic species may resemble oyster mushrooms.

3. Lentinula edodes (Shiitake Mushroom)

- Shiitake mushrooms are highly valued for their rich, savory flavor, often described as umami.
- They are widely used in Asian cuisine, including stir-fries, soups, and stews, and as an ingredient in traditional medicine.
- Shiitake mushrooms contain compounds with potential health benefits, such as lentinan, which is known for its immunomodulatory properties.
- While generally safe to eat, some individuals may experience mild digestive discomfort if consuming raw or undercooked shiitake mushrooms. Cooking them thoroughly is recommended.

4. Hericium erinaceus (Lion's Mane Mushroom)

- Lion's Mane mushrooms have a delicate, seafood-like flavor and a texture resembling crab or lobster meat.
- They can be cooked in various ways, such as sautéing, stir-frying, or incorporating them into soups and stews.

- Lion's Mane mushrooms have gained attention for their potential neuroprotective effects and their ability to support cognitive health.
- While generally considered safe to eat, some individuals may experience mild allergies or digestive discomfort. It is recommended to cook them thoroughly before consumption.

5. Cantharellus cibarius (Chanterelle Mushroom)

- Chanterelle mushrooms are highly prized for their fruity, apricot-like flavor and their meaty yet delicate texture.
- They are sought after by chefs and foragers alike and are used in various culinary creations, including sauces, soups, risottos, and sautés.
- Chanterelles are rich in vitamins, minerals, and dietary fiber.
- It is essential to properly identify chanterelle mushrooms, as some toxic look-alike species exist. If uncertain, it is advisable to consult an experienced mushroom identifier before consumption.

6. Ganoderma lucidum (Reishi Mushroom)

- Reishi mushrooms are used for their potential immune-enhancing properties, as well as for their antioxidant and anti-inflammatory effects. They are also believed to support stress reduction and promote overall well-being.
- Reishi mushrooms are generally considered safe for most individuals when consumed as a food or supplement. However, individuals taking blood-thinning medications or with low blood pressure should exercise caution, as Reishi may have anticoagulant and hypotensive effects. It's advisable to consult with a healthcare professional before using Reishi as a supplement.

7. Cordyceps sinensis (Caterpillar Fungus)

- Cordyceps mushrooms are known for their potential adaptogenic properties, supporting energy, endurance, and athletic performance. They are also used to support respiratory health and immune function.
- Cordyceps mushrooms are generally considered safe for consumption. However, it's advisable to purchase Cordyceps products from reputable sources, as there are rare cases of counterfeit or adulterated products on the market. People with autoimmune conditions or bleeding disorders should consult with a healthcare professional before using Cordyceps.

8. Trametes versicolor (Turkey Tail Mushroom)

- Turkey Tail mushrooms are used for their potential immunomodulatory effects and are often used as adjunctive therapy for cancer. They are also believed to have antioxidant properties and may support overall immune health.

- Turkey Tail mushrooms are generally considered safe for consumption. However, individuals with autoimmune diseases or those taking immunosuppressive medications should exercise caution and consult with a healthcare professional before using Turkey Tail as a supplement.

9. Inonotus obliquus (Chaga Mushroom)

- Chaga mushrooms have a long history of use in traditional medicine, particularly in Siberian and Eastern European cultures.
- They are highly regarded for their potential health benefits and are often consumed as tea or used in extracts, tinctures, or powders.
- Chaga mushrooms are rich in antioxidants, such as melanin and phenolic compounds, which contribute to their potential health-promoting properties.
- They are believed to have potential anticancer, anti-inflammatory, immune-enhancing, and skin-protective effects.
- While generally considered safe for most individuals, it is recommended to source Chaga mushrooms from reputable suppliers and consult with a healthcare professional before use, especially if you have any underlying health conditions or are taking medications.

10. Grifola frondosa (Maitake Mushroom)

- Maitake mushrooms are known for their potential immune-enhancing and antitumor effects. They are used to support overall immune health and may have general wellness benefits.
- Maitake mushrooms are generally safe for consumption. However, individuals with autoimmune diseases or those taking immunosuppressive medications should exercise caution and consult with a healthcare professional before using Maitake as a supplement.

CONCLUSION

As we draw the curtains on this enlightening journey through the world of mushroom cultivation, we hope this guide, *Mushroom Cultivation for Beginners*, has served as a beacon, illuminating the pathway to your own fruitful mushroom garden. We have traveled through the biology of mushrooms, explored their varied types, delved into the nitty-gritty of home cultivation, and even ventured into the realm of exotic varieties and commercial production.

The essence of this book, however, goes far beyond the how-to's and techniques. It extends to a deeper philosophy, one that emphasizes connection—with nature, with our food, and, most importantly, with each other. This shared hobby of mushroom cultivation is not just an activity; it's a conduit for enriching relationships, bonding over common interests, and igniting sparks of curiosity, especially in the minds of younger family members.

We trust that the practical knowledge acquired from this book will empower you to establish your own mushroom growing area, whether it be a cozy corner in your home or a dedicated outdoor space. May the troubleshooting tips come to your rescue during challenging times, helping you overcome common diseases and pests that might otherwise hinder your progress.

We hoped to inspire gastronomes and families alike with a delectable array of recipes showcasing the culinary versatility of mushrooms. Remember that each dish prepared with your home-grown mushrooms is a celebration of your patience, effort, and connection to the food you consume.

Looking forward, for those with an adventurous spirit or entrepreneurial mind, we hope that the sections on advanced cultivation techniques and commercial mushroom farming have sparked further interest. The fascinating world of mushrooms is indeed wide and deep, full of opportunities for exploration and growth.

Remember that every new spore you plant, every mushroom you nurture to fruition, and every bite you enjoy from your harvest contributes to a greater understanding of our place in nature's grand tapestry.

Keep exploring, keep cultivating, and most importantly, keep growing not just mushrooms but also bonds, knowledge, and a deeper respect for the natural world around us. Happy mushroom cultivating!

Made in the USA
Las Vegas, NV
15 November 2023

80878902R00070